Bento Blast!

MORE THAN 150 CUTE AND CLEVER BENTO BOX MEALS FOR YOUR KIDS

LI MING LEE

Racehorse Publishing

Copyright © 2015, 2019 by Li Ming Lee

All rights reserved. No part of this book may be reproduced in any manner without the express written consent of the publisher, except in the case of brief excerpts in critical reviews or articles. All inquiries should be addressed to Skyhorse Publishing, 307 West 36th Street, 11th Floor, New York, NY 10018.

Racehorse Publishing books may be purchased in bulk at special discounts for sales promotion, corporate gifts, fund-raising, or educational purposes. Special editions can also be created to specifications. For details, contact the Special Sales Department, Skyhorse Publishing, 307 West 36th Street, 11th Floor, New York, NY 10018 or info@skyhorsepublishing.com.

Racehorse Publishing™ is a pending trademark of Skyhorse Publishing, Inc.®, a Delaware corporation.

Visit our website at www.skyhorsepublishing.com.

10 9 8 7 6 5 4 3

Library of Congress Cataloging-in-Publication Data is available on file.

Cover and interior photographs by Li Ming Lee

Print ISBN: 978-1-63158-465-7
Ebook ISBN: 978-1-63158-466-4

Printed in China

Previously published as *Yummy Kawaii Bento* (978-1-63450-424-9)

Contents

Introduction vii

What Is Bento? 1

Bento Boxes 2

Bento Making Tools 5

Bento Making Techniques 10

Bento Packing Basics 18

Be Creative! 22

Bento and Food Art Tutorials 23

Rice-Based Bentos 23

Piggy Onigiri 24

Sheep in a Meadow 26

Relaxing Panda 29

Ice Cream Buddies 32

Baby Bear 34

Bunny and Sunflower 36

Penguin Onigiri 38

Baby Pandas 40

Puffer Fish 42

Soboro Lion 44

Scrambled Eggs Clown 46

Ninjas 48

Baby Inari Sushi 50

Witch 52

Sleeping Kitty Cat 54

Hot Dog Bear Sushi 56

Scrambled Eggs Chick 58

Tomato Ladybugs 60

Piggy Spam Musubi 62

Koala Onigiri 64

Bread-Based Bentos 67

Bear Sandwich Rolls 68

Penguin Sandwich 70

Piggy Pocket Sandwich 72

Snail Sandwich 74

Mashed Potato Duck
Sandwich 76

Animal Bread Balls 78

Chicks in Bread Cup Nests 81

Hot Dog Bunnies 84

Bunny Carrot 86

Seal Sandwich 88

Mermaid 90

Sleeping Teddy Bear
Sandwich 92

Cat and Yarn Pita 94

Piggy Chicken Wrap 96

Bread Car 98

Tiger Bread Buns 100

Hot Dog Bread Bun 102

Owl Bread Buns 104

Dog Burger 106

Astronaut 108

Salad and Noodle Bentos 111

Sleeping Bunny Salad 112

Cow Salad 114

Quail Egg Mice 116

Pesto Pasta Frog 118

Meatball Pasta Bear 120

Shrimp Snail Pad Thai 122

Special Occasions 124

Sushi Birthday Cake 125

Mother's Day Hen and
   Chicks 128
Father's Day 130
Christmas Santa 132
Wintery Snowman 134
Spooky Halloween 136
Halloween Monster and Mummy
   Sandwich 138
Easter Chicks in Bunny Suits 140
Valentine's Day Rose Wrap 143
Back to School 146
Seasonal Bentos 148
Spring Sunflower Bee 149
Summer Girl 152
Fall Squirrel 154
Winter Girl 156
Raincoat Bear 158
Sunny Day by the Beach 160
Night Time 163
Food Art 167
Curry Polar Bear 168
Swimming Ducky 170
Ham Piggy 172
Puff Pastry Soup Bear 174
Soup Kitty 176
Tomato Soup Owl 178
Pizza Bear 180
Animal Tortilla Chips 182
Bonus Food Art Recipes 185
Hot Dog Bread 186
Steamed Chick Cake 189
Bunny German Cookies 192
Steamed Piggy Buns 194
Bear Cream Puff 197

Recipes 201
Meat 201
Seaweed Pork Rolls 202
Japanese Beef Curry 202
Chicken Nuggets 203
White Wine Chicken Stew 203
Chicken Veggie Roll 204
Chicken Teriyaki 205
Pork Nuggets 205
Veggie Pork/Beef Rolls 206
Chinese Pork Chops 206
Ketchup Pork Chops 207
Brown Sauce Pork Chops 207
Grilled Chicken Balls 208
Cajun Spiced Grilled Wings 208
Chicken Carrot Stir-Fry 209
Chicken Salad 209
Chicken Tofu Patties 210
Chicken Milk Stew 211
Ground Pork and Potato
   Stir-Fry 211
Lemon Chicken 212
Tonkatsu 212
Black Pepper Chicken 213
Chicken Veggie Stir-Fry 213
Honey Chicken 214
Meat Soboro 215
Crispy Chicken Fillet 215
Pork Carrot Patties 216
Pork Cabbage Stir-Fry 216
Japanese Hamburg Steak 217
Seafood and Egg 218
Ketchup Shrimp 219
Fried Salmon Belly Fingers 219
Garlic Shrimp 220

Crispy Fried Shrimp 220
Salmon Mayonnaise 221
Cheesy Fish Fillet 221
Salted Salmon 222
Lemon Soy Sauce Salmon 222
Lemon Dill Salmon 223
Cheese Baked Shrimp 223
Scrambled Eggs 224
Green Bean Omelette 224
Tamagoyaki 225
Vegetables 226
Sesame Broccoli 227
Zucchini and Tomato Baked with
    Cheese 227
Bell Peppers Stir-Fry 227
Squash Stir-Fry 228
Sriracha Asparagus 228
Potato Salad 228
Broccoli Pasta Salad 229
Green Beans and Mushroom
    Stir-Fry 229
Butter Mushrooms 230

Broccoli and Carrot
    Stir-Fry 230
Soy Sauce Okra 230
Sesame Spinach 231
Pea Shoots and Mushroom
    Stir-Fry 231
Asparagus and Corn Stir-Fry 231
Noodles and Soup 232
Chicken Carbonara 233
Seafood Aglio e Olio 233
Meatball Pasta 234
Chicken Bolognese Pasta 235
Pad Thai 236
Pesto Pasta 237
Curry Pumpkin Soup 237
Asparagus Soup 238
Tomato Soup 238

Glossary 239
Templates 246
Acknowledgments 247
About the Author 248

Introduction

I started making character bentos when my firstborn began elementary school in 2011. He had problems adapting to the longer hours at school. He missed me and cried when I sent him to school every day. I started packing him character bentos, along with lunch notes, in order to cheer him up and let him feel my love and presence through them.

I started my blog, www.bentomonsters.com, in August 2011 because I wanted a platform to journal down the character bentos I made for my boys. One day, when they are grown up, I hope that they will be able to look back on the blog and recall the fond memories they had of their character bentos when they were little. Over time, making character bentos has also become a personal hobby, which I enjoy whenever I have pockets of free time. I intend to continue to make character bentos for as long as my boys are willing to eat them.

I've always wanted to write a book as I thought it would be the perfect keepsake for my bento making journey. In addition, when I first started making character bentos, most of the character bento making books available were written in Japanese. I'd always felt that it would have been great to have one in English that would cover all the basic character bento making techniques. This is what I'm trying to do now, even though I'm no professional in this arena and am still learning every day! I hope to share with you everything I've learnt through trial and error these few years.

This book encompasses all the basic character making techniques needed to get you started, lots of bento designs, complete with step-by-step pictures, as well as bento food recipes to guide you along. I've tried to keep most of the designs simple, so it's easy for you to recreate them. I hope that this book will inspire you to try your hand at making your own character bentos—and I hope you will enjoy the process as much as I do.

What Is Bento?

Bento simply means "meal packed in a box." It is very popular in Japan and is in fact an integral part of the culture. Bentos can be bought in many places throughout Japan, including convenience stores, bento shops, railway stations, and department stores. Bentos can also be homemade. In Japan, it is common for children to bring bentos to school and for adults to bring bentos to work for lunch. Over the past few years, bento culture has gained popularity worldwide and there has been a global spread of bento to different parts of the world. It is especially interesting to see how bentos have evolved and adapted in different countries, cultures, and communities.

Character bento, or charaben, is a type of bento that features food decorated and styled to look like people, animals, characters from cartoons, etc. Character bentos started as a way for parents to encourage their picky kids to eat a wider range of foods, especially healthy food. Mothers in Japan often pack character bentos for their children who go to kindergarten.

I believe that in making a character bento, the taste of the bento should not be compromised for its presentation. It is important to prepare a wholesome meal so that the bento tastes as good as it looks. I also believe that making a character bento should not take up too much of your time. As a result, I've simplified a majority of the character bentos I'm sharing in this book so that they are quick and easy to create. I've also included a recipe section in this book, so you can recreate the dishes that make up my bentos. With a little effort and some creativity, a bento will not only bring a smile to its recipient's face, but will also become an enjoyable process for the maker.

Whenever you prepare character bentos, it helps to plan in advance what you would like to make. This way, you can have all the ingredients ready beforehand, which will make the job much easier. Bento tools like a nori punch, cutters, or a rice mold are useful and will also save time in character bento making. However, refrain from buying and overloading on too many tools if you are starting out on your bento making journey. Most of the basic tools needed to get you started can be found in your kitchen, such as cling wrap, scissors, knives, toothpicks, etc. It's better to try your hand at making character bentos first and slowly ascertain what tools you would need the most, before making your purchases.

Bento Boxes

Bento boxes come in all sorts of shapes and sizes. They are also made from different kinds of materials. In choosing a bento box, you will need to look at your meal serving requirements. Generally speaking, for a tightly packed Japanese-style bento (following the rule of three parts grain dishes, one part protein dishes, and two parts vegetable dishes), the number of milliliters (ml) that a box can hold corresponds roughly to the number of calories it holds. As a guide, a child needs a 400–600ml (13.5–20 oz) bento box. A female needs around 600ml (20 oz) and a male needs around 900ml (30.5 oz). This is just a rough guide, and you may need to add more food for those who engage in higher physical activity or reduce food for those with lower physical activity. The chart below shows a more detailed guide according to age.

WOMEN

Age	Bento Box Size (ml)	(oz)
3–5	400	13.5
6–8	500	17
9–11	600	20
12–17	700	23.5
30–60	600	20
70–80	500	17

MEN

Age	Bento Box Size (ml)	(oz)
3–5	400	13.5
6–8	500	17
9–11	600	20
12–40	900	30.5
50–60	800	27
70–80	600	20

Bentos are great for portion control. They allow you to choose the appropriate bento box size according to your dietary needs, and all you have to do is pack food in the bento box.

Here is a guide to most of the bento boxes I used in this book:

PLASTIC BENTO BOXES

Plastic boxes should be BPA-free. If you need to reheat your bento box, make sure your bento box is microwave safe.

Bento boxes can come with compartments. This ensures that food does not touch and makes packing easy.

If you are packing something with sauce, you will need an airtight box to prevent the sauce from spilling.

Boxes with attached lids are suitable for younger kids, especially if you have an absentminded kid. You will not have to worry about your child forgetting about and leaving their lids at school.

Bento boxes with cute characters are more attractive to kids.

Where to get them: www.bentousa.com, en.bentoandco.com, us.monbento.com/en, www.easylunchboxes.com.

Some bento boxes come with built-in gel lids. If you freeze the gel lid overnight, it will keep your bento cool until lunchtime.

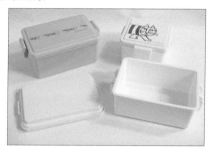

Foldable sandwich boxes can be folded up after lunch, thus saving space. They also save space when they are being stored.

MAGEWAPPA (BENTWOOD) AND WOODEN BENTO BOXES

These boxes are very beautiful and are great for packing rice. The wood allows the rice to breathe and makes plain rice taste wonderful. Food might stain the wood, so it's better to line the boxes with wax paper or food cups when packing. These are costly and might be more suitable for older children who can take better care of their belongings.

Where to get them: en.bentoandco.com

METAL BENTO BOXES

Metal bento boxes are mostly made from aluminum and stainless steel. They are very durable and easy to clean. Metal does not absorb the flavors and odors of food like plastic does; however, do note that metal containers are not microwavable, although high quality ones may be heated up in ovens. Most aluminum bento boxes have loose, unsecured lids, held together using a band. Because of this, you should only pack drier food in these boxes.

If you need a leakproof metal box, look for stainless steel bento boxes that come with a silicon seal inside the rim.

Where to get them: en.bentoandco.com, www.bentousa.com, www.black-blum.com

THERMAL CONTAINERS

Bentos are traditionally eaten at room temperature. If you prefer a warm lunch and have no heating facilities available at lunch time, a thermal food jar will be a good choice. However, do take note that food continues to cook in thermal containers, so choose food that benefits from slow cooking. Suitable items to pack include stews, soup, curries, or rice. For young kids, do take extra precaution by informing their teachers to help them to open the jar, in case the hot contents spill out.

Where to get them: www.bentousa.com, en.bentoandco.com

Bento Making Tools

CLING WRAP

This is an important tool to help you make rice balls. Using cling wrap prevents rice from sticking to your hands. With the help of cling wrap, you can easily mold rice into different shapes. Learn the basic technique on shaping rice using cling wrap (p. 13). When wrapping rice or eggs with nori, wrapping it with cling wrap will also help the nori to adhere to the rice or eggs. You can get cling wrap at any grocery store.

NORI PUNCHES

Even though you can cut out most decorative shapes from seaweed, also called nori, using a pair of scissors, a nori punch is useful for cutting out smaller and more precise shapes like circles and ovals. Nori punches are specifically designed for cutting sheets of nori.

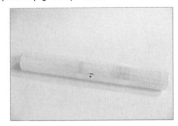

Paper punches, found at craft stores, can also be used to cut seaweed.

When choosing nori, get unseasoned nori as it can keep better after opening. Choosing a thicker, better quality nori will give you a darker, almost black cutout, whereas thinner nori sheets tend to give greenish cutouts. After opening a packet of nori, you can cut it up into smaller pieces and keep it in an airtight container with a desiccant.

Where to get them: www.bentousa.com, en.bentoandco.com, craft stores

TWEEZERS

Tweezers with sharp tips are useful in handling and adjusting more intricate bento details. Some tweezers are made especially for bento making. You can also use tweezers made for bead craft.

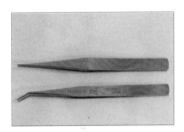

Where to get them: www.bentousa.com, craft stores

SCISSORS

A pair of small, sharp-tipped scissors is an essential item in character bento making. It will help you to make precise cuts of small decorative parts.

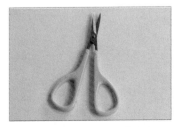

Where to get them: www.bentousa.com, craft stores

CUTTERS

Even though most decorative parts in character bento making can be cut freehand, using a cutter makes the job faster and easier. Cutters come in different shapes and sizes.

Some cutters are specially designed for bento use. These cutters are more suitable for cutting softer ingredients like ham, bread, and cheese.

Cutters used for cutting vegetables are great for bento. These cutters can be made of metal or plastic. The cutters are more durable and can cut harder and thicker ingredients like carrots before they are cooked.

You can look for cutters in bakeware stores too. These cutters, which come in plastic and metal, are originally designed for cutting cookies and/or fondant, but they can double as bento making tools.

Sandwich cutters, which are bigger in size, are used for cutting bread into fun shapes. Some of them come along with a stamper, which can be used to make imprints on the bread. There are also sandwich cutters with molds—these seal up the edges of the sandwich so its fillings inside will not fall out.

Everyday household items can also be used as cutters. Keep a variety of different sized straws, snip them short, and use them to cut out circles. You can use them to cut out ovals too, simply by squeezing the straw into an oval shape while you make the cut. The front of round piping tips and the back of all piping tips can double up as circle cutters too.

Where to get them: www.bentousa.com, baking supplies stores

BENTO PICKS

Bento picks are a quick way to decorate bentos. They add an instant touch of cuteness to the food. There are lots of varieties out there and you will be spoiled for choice. They are functional as well, and are used to skewer foods like meatballs, edamame, and fruits.

You can make homemade picks with the help of decorative washi tape (also available in scrapbooking sections at Michaels or Walmart) and toothpicks.

You can also check out baking supplies stores for cupcake toppers to decorate your bento. Do note that these toppers tend to be larger in size compared to bento picks.

I like to store my bento picks in plastic boxes with compartments. It's easier to organize, and it helps when I need to pick out the ones I want to use.

Where to get them: www.bentousa.com, en.bentoandco, baking supplies stores

WAX PAPER

Wax paper is useful in lining wooden bento boxes and sandwich boxes. It can also be used to wrap sandwiches and separate foods in the bento box. It come in a variety of prints and designs. You can match the wax paper with the theme of your bento.

Where to get them: www.bentousa.com, en.bentoandco.com

CUTTING KNIVES

These are used to make precise cuts on ingredients. They are especially useful for cutting out food from a template (p. 17). These knifes are usually used for arts and crafts projects.

Where to get them: craft stores

RICE MOLDS

Rice molds come in a variety of shapes, from traditional shapes like circles and triangles to more specific images of animals and flowers. Rice molds make it easy to mold rice into different shapes and are useful for beginners. They are also useful when you need to make a large quantity of rice balls and you want to be consistent with your sizes and shapes.

Where to get them: www.bentousa.com, en.bentoandco.com

FOOD CUPS

Food cups help to keep the rice and side dishes in your box separate, so they don't mix with each other. It also helps to prevent the food from staining your bento box. Food cups can be made from silicon or plastic and are reusable. Good quality silicon food cups can be used in the oven, microwave, steamer, or freezer as they can withstand extreme temperatures such as a high of 446°F (230°C) and a low of -40°F (-40°C)—but please read usage instructions as this may vary.

Food cups can also be made from paper and aluminum. These are not reusable.

Where to get them: www.bentousa.com, en.bentoandco.com

SAUCE BOTTLES/CONTAINERS

Sauce bottles are usually used for soy sauce, while containers are used for sauces like ketchup, mayonnaise, or salad dressing.

Where to get them: www.bentousa.com, en.bentoandco.com, us.monbento.com/en, www.easylunchboxes.com

BARANS

These are used to keep side dishes separate, and are more useful for dry foods, as food with sauce can still flow underneath them. Barans come in different designs and can be used to decorate your bento box as well. They can be made from plastic film sheets or silicon.

Where to get them: www.bentousa.com, en.bentoandco.com

EGG MOLDS

Eggs can be molded into different shapes when they are still warm. Egg molds come in different shapes and designs. Place a hot/warm boiled egg into the egg mold and immerse the mold in cold water until the egg has cooled down. This will give you a molded egg.

Where to get them: www.bentousa.com, en.bentoandco.com, us.monbento.com/en

GEL PACKS

Gel packs are used to keep your lunch cool until lunchtime. When you pop them in the freezer overnight, the gel will turn to ice and you can place them on top of your bento box. Be careful not to make any holes in them—discard them if that happens. Do not let the gel pack/ice pack come into direct contact with the food.

Where to get them: www.bentousa.com, en.bentoandco.com

Bento Making Techniques

COLORING RICE

There are many different ways to color rice. The most convenient way would be using deco-furi, sushi mix, or sakura denbu, which are rice seasoning condiments that also add color to the rice when mixed in.

Deco-furi

Sushi mix

Sakura denbu

When mixing deco-furi with rice, do it while the rice is still hot or warm. The more deco-furi added, the brighter the color will be. Please note that deco-furi will make the rice salty, so avoid adding too much. Another good way to use deco-furi would be to wrap a plain rice ball inside an outer layer of colored rice. This way, the rice won't be too salty but the color will still be vibrant.

Sushi mix and sakura denbu can be used to color rice a sweet pinkish shade.

A healthier option would be to color your rice using natural food ingredients. You will be surprised at the beautiful colors you can achieve just by using natural foods.

To get you started, here is a list of ingredients that can be used to produce certain colors to dye your rice. This list is non-exhaustive, and with experimentation you may discover more natural food dyes. As a general rule, fresh ingredients can be boiled or steamed, then mashed to produce the dye.

RED

Beetroot

Ketchup

PINK

Beetroot

BROWN

Dark soy sauce

Teriyaki sauce

GREY

Ground black sesame

GREEN

Peas

Edamame

Spinach

YELLOW

Egg yolk

Scrambled eggs

PURPLE

Purple potato

Red cabbage

BLUE

Butterfly pea flower water

Red cabbage water with baking soda added

ORANGE

Squash seeds

Carrots

SHAPING RICE USING RICE MOLD

There are many different types of rice molds available, but the method to use each of them is similar. The type of rice that is most suitable to be molded is short grained rice, as it's sticky when cooked and it holds its shape well. For this demonstration, I used a penguin-shaped rice mold to shape my rice.

1. Dip the rice mold in water before using to prevent rice from sticking to mold. Fill the mold with rice. If you want fillings in your rice, fill in half the mold with rice first, add the fillings, and finally top the mold with more rice.

2. Press the lid on tightly.

3. Remove the lid, turn the mold over, and tap lightly so that the rice will fall out. Your rice is now ready to be used.

4. Some rice mold sets, like the one I'm using, come with a seaweed cutter. Simply place the seaweed on the cutting mat provided in the set and press on the cutter to cut through the seaweed.

SHAPING RICE USING CLING WRAP

Cling wrap is the most versatile way to shape rice. It gives you more flexibility compared to a rice mold. Once again, short grained rice is preferred as it holds its shape better.

1. Place cling wrap on your palm and scoop rice on it.

2. If you want to add filling, scoop filling onto the center of the rice. Skip this step if you want to leave your rice plain.

3. Bring the ends of the cling wrap together. Twist the ends to tighten as you shape the rice into a compact rice ball.

4. Use your hands to mold the rice into different shapes while it is still wrapped in the cling wrap.

MAKING EGG SHEETS

An egg sheet is, essentially, a colored sheet that is made from eggs. Egg sheets can be cut using a scissors or a knife to form character shapes (p. 17) or to be used to make various decorations like sunflowers, blankets, and raincoats. To make colored egg sheets, use gel-based food coloring as they will not thin your egg mixture. You can make egg sheets in advance and freeze them—just sandwich the egg sheet with cling wrap and put it in a ziplock bag.

YELLOW EGG SHEET

INGREDIENTS

1 egg
½ tsp cornstarch
1 tsp water

METHOD:

1. Beat egg with whisk or fork in a bowl.

2. Add ½ tsp cornstarch to 1 tsp water. Add the cornstarch mixture to the egg.

3. Strain the egg mixture. This step is very important to get rid of the bubbles so that we can get a smooth egg sheet.

4. Use a tamagoyaki pan or a rectangular pan to create your rectangular egg sheet. Put a little cooking oil in and wipe the surface with kitchen towels.

5. Pour a thin layer of mixture into the pan right after you put the pan on the stove. Turn on the stove at low heat.

6. Once the top layer starts to harden, turn off the stove and let the egg sheet continue to cook for a while. Remove and transfer to a plate or cutting board using a spatula. If the egg sheet was cooked in a round pan, trim off the edges to form a square.

WHITE OR COLORED EGG SHEET

INGREDIENTS

2 egg whites
½ tsp cornstarch

1 tsp water
Gel-based food coloring

METHOD:

1. Beat egg whites with whisk or fork in a bowl.

2. Add ½ tsp cornstarch to 1 tsp water. If you would like to color the egg sheet, add the coloring to the cornstarch mixture. Add the cornstarch mixture to the egg.

3. Strain the egg mixture. This step is very important to get rid of the bubbles so that we can get a smooth egg sheet.

4. Put a little cooking oil on a tamagoyaki pan. Use kitchen towels to wipe the surface.

5. Pour a thin layer of mixture into the pan right after you put the pan on the stove. Turn on the stove at low heat.

6. Once the top layer starts to harden, turn off the stove and let the egg sheet continue to cook for a while. Remove and transfer to a plate or cutting board using a spatula.

COLORING HARD-BOILED EGGS

Hard-boiled eggs can be used to decorate your bento or made into different characters and designs. They can be colored by soaking them in water that has been dyed with either artificial food coloring or natural ingredients. Here, I will share some ways to prepare different colored dye solutions using natural ingredients. The stronger colors, like beets and turmeric, set pretty quickly, but you'll want to keep the others soaking longer to achieve a brighter color.

Bring water to boil. Place room temperature chicken eggs in the pot and boil for 6–7 minutes. Reduce the time if you are making hard-boiled quail eggs. Remove hard-boiled eggs and peel them. Immediately, place them in the dye solution and soak until you get your desired color.

PREPARING DYE SOLUTIONS

- **Purple–red:** Boil beets and puree them. Strain and reserve liquids.
- **Light pink:** Use strained beet juice straight from the can or water leftover from boiling beets.
- **Yellow:** Mix turmeric or curry powder with hot water.
- **Green:** Mix green tea powder, also called matcha, with hot water.
- **Brown:** Add soy sauce to water.
- **Blue:** Shred red cabbage and boil it in water. Strain and reserve liquids.
- **Purple:** Use purple grape juice that you can find on the shelves in any grocery store.
- **Orange:** Mix turmeric powder with hot water. Slowly add strained beet juice until you get a dark orange color.

CUTTING CHARACTERS FROM A TEMPLATE

Some of the ingredients you can use for this method are cheese, ham, egg sheets, bread, and aburaage (a product made from soybeans).

1. Draw or print out the design you want on a piece of paper. Trace out the picture using parchment paper.

2. Decide on the different layers you want for your character (layers will make them "pop up") and trace them out on parchment paper as well.

3. Cut out the different parts on the parchment paper using scissors or a cutting knife.

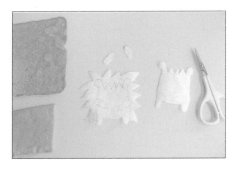

4. Lay out the paper cutouts on your food ingredients. Using a cutting knife, cut along the outline of the paper. If you are making cutouts in cheese, a toothpick can be used too.

5. Assemble the different layers you have cut out to complete your design. Add further details, such as the eyes, nose, and mouth, using nori cutouts.

Bento Packing Basics

Bento should have a good mix of carbohydrates, proteins, fruits, and vegetables. Bento is usually eaten at room temperature, so the food that you pack in it should still taste good when slightly cold.

When packing food that may have to sit at room temperature for some time before it is eaten, it is crucial to follow proper, safe bento-packing practices. Wash your hands to ensure they are clean before packing. Try to handle the food with your bare hands as little as possible—use chopsticks and other utensils to arrange your food. Make sure food has fully cooled down before closing the bento lid. In warmer weather or for food that might spoil easily, be sure to use a gel pack (p. 9).

In order to prevent the bento contents from shifting during transport and ruining your efforts, make sure that the food is packed tightly without any gaps in between. Some examples of food that are well suited to fill small gaps in your bento box are broccoli, cherry tomatoes, rolled up ham, sausages, grapes, and strawberries. We call them bento fillers.

1. Have the food, bento box, and bento tools ready before you start packing.

2. For bento boxes like magewappa (wooden bentos), which are prone to staining, line with wax paper first. Place lettuce in the bento box and place rice balls in a silicon cup to prevent them from shifting or mixing with other food.

3. Place side dishes in food cups to prevent food flavors from mingling.

4. Pack the main dish that has a fixed shape to fit in the container first.

5. Then, continue to pack in the other side dishes.

6. Fill in the empty space with fillers, in this case, broccoli. And you're done!

Pasta sticks are used as "edible toothpicks" to secure character details in place. This prevents the details from shifting when the bento box is being transported. The raw pasta sticks will absorb moisture from other food ingredients in the bento and soften by lunchtime, so they will be safe for consumption. If you are planning to eat your creations immediately after preparation, you can also fry them in a little oil until they turn brown and crispy.

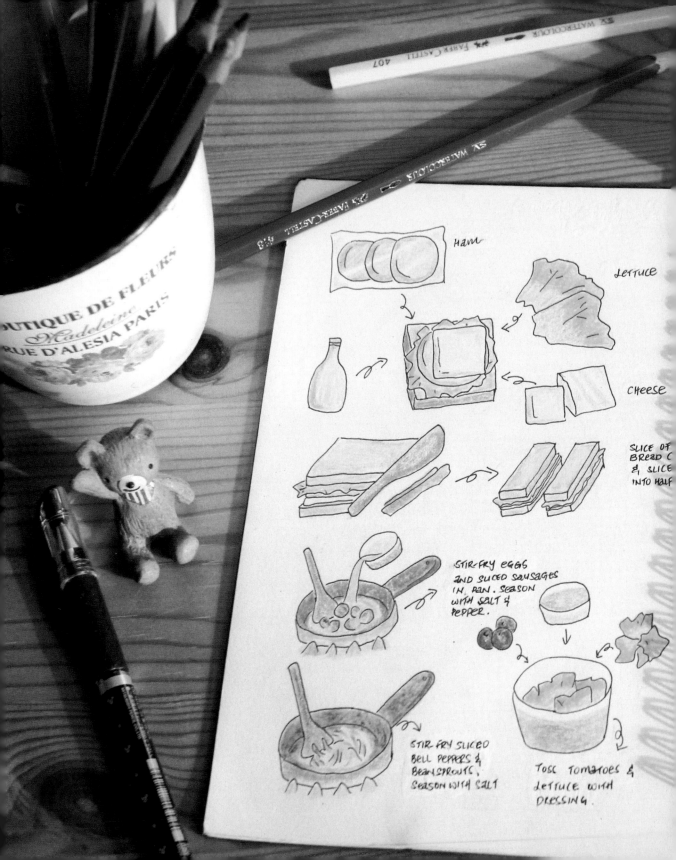

Ham

Lettuce

Cheese

Slice of
Bread C
& Slice
into half

Stir-fry eggs
and sliced sausages
in pan. Season
with salt &
pepper.

Stir-fry sliced
bell peppers &
beansprouts,
season with salt

Toss tomatoes &
lettuce with
dressing.

LETTUCE & CHERRY TOMATOES

SAUSAGE & EGGS

BELL PEPPERS & BEANSPROUTS

HAM & CHEESE SANDWICH

Be Creative!

Before we begin, it is most important to note that character bento making is about using your creativity and imagination. Even as you follow my bento tutorials in the following pages, remember that they are not set in stone. Instead, think of them as a guide and feel free to mix and match recipes and methods according to your own preferences! Experiment, try out different permutations and combinations, and very soon you should feel comfortable making your very own bento box creations.

In these tutorials, "bento menu" lists the recipes that I used to make the bento's side dishes, "food art ingredients" lists the ingredients used to design and make the characters, and "tools needed" lists the equipment that you will need. Recipes for the side dishes can be found in a separate recipe section at the back of the book (p. 201).

Be creative, and have fun!

Bento and Food Art Tutorials

RICE-BASED BENTOS

Piggy Onigiri

A smiley piggy onigiri (a rice ball) is so easy to make. Learn to make not one but two kawaii piggies for this bento—a large piggy made from rice and a mini piggy made from a quail egg. This bento also includes salmon belly that has been cut into strips and coated with cornmeal before frying.

BENTO MENU

Chicken nuggets (p. 203)
Fried salmon belly fingers
    (p. 219)
Tamagoyaki (p. 225)
Blanched broccoli
Cherry tomato
Lettuce

FOOD ART INGREDIENTS

Rice
Nori
Ham
Ketchup
Quail egg
Pasta sticks

TOOLS NEEDED

Cling wrap
Food cup
Tweezers
Scissors
Straws/round cutters
Hole punch
Paw craft punch
Chopstick
Panda bento picks

1. Place rice on cling wrap, wrap it up, and shape into an oval rice ball. Place rice in a food cup. Cut out piggy's ears and snout from the ham using a pair of scissors.

2. Using a straw, cut two holes into the ham meant for the snout.

3. Attach the ham cutouts onto the rice using pasta sticks.

4. Using a hole punch, cut out two circles from a sheet of nori. Cut out a curved line from the nori for the mouth with a pair of scissors.

5. Dab on ketchup for the cheeks using a chopstick.

6. Prepare a hard-boiled quail egg. Cut out piggy's ears and snout again from the ham using a pair of scissors. Attach the ham cutouts onto the quail egg using pasta sticks.

7. Using a craft punch, cut out the pig's eyes from a sheet of nori.

8. Arrange food in the bento box. Separate food with the help of lettuce and food cups.

Sheep in a Meadow

A pair of fluffy white sheep sleep on a bed of alfalfa sprouts. Here, you will also learn to make tomato roses that will make a quick decoration for any bento. This bento also includes veggie pork rolls, which are made from carrots and asparagus that are rolled with thinly sliced pork (it can also be made with beef). They not only look pretty in your bento, but also taste yummy and are a great way to encourage picky eaters to eat more veggies.

BENTO MENU	FOOD ART INGREDIENTS	TOOLS NEEDED
Veggie pork/beef rolls (p. 206)	Rice	Cling wrap
Tamagoyaki (p. 225)	Ketchup	Tweezers
Alfafa sprouts	Ham	Knife
Lettuce	Egg sheet	Scissors
	Nori	Nori punch
	Black olives	Oval cutter
	Tomato	Vegetable peeler
	Pasta sticks	Sheep bento picks

1. Color rice using a little ketchup. Using cling wrap, form two rice balls—one small oval for the head and one big oval for the body.

2. Place the small rice ball on top of the big one and secure together using pasta sticks.

3. Using cling wrap, arrange more white rice loosely over the rice ball so that it looks like the fluffy wool of the sheep.

4. Slice olives and cut them into small ovals for the nose. Using a pair of scissors, cut out two curved lines from a sheet of nori for the mouths. Use a nori punch to cut out the eyes from the nori.

5. To make the curled horns of the sheep, cut out a long strip from an egg sheet, roll it up, and secure it to the sheep's head with pasta sticks.

6. Using an oval cutter, cut out oval shapes from ham and attach onto the sheep using pasta sticks. These form the sheep's rosy cheeks.

7. Using a peeler or a knife, slice out a strip of tomato skin.

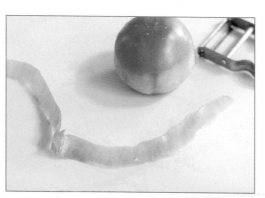

8. Roll up the tomato skins together and you will soon see a rose forming. Tuck the ends in when you are done.

Relaxing Panda

A relaxing panda takes a stretch in a beautiful magewappa bento box. This panda is surrounded by yummy, crispy fried shrimp, stir-fried chicken and carrots, and scallion tamagoyaki. Scallion provides a variation to the basic tamagoyaki recipe. You can come up with more variations by adding chopped carrots, spinach, or imitation crab meat. Also, learn to cut out pretty 3-D carrot flowers seen in this bento by following the step-by-step photos.

BENTO MENU
Chicken carrot stir-fry
   (p. 209)
Crispy fried shrimp
   (p. 220)
Scallion tamagoyaki
   (p. 225)
Edamame
Lettuce

FOOD ART INGREDIENTS
Rice
Nori
Carrots
Pasta sticks

TOOLS NEEDED
Cling wrap
Food cup
Tweezers
Scissors
Oval-shaped cutter
Flower-shaped cutter
Knife
Panda bento picks

1. Scoop rice onto cling wrap. Secure cling wrap by twisting the ends and shape into an oval rice ball for the panda's body. Repeat and shape another one.

2. Place the rice balls into food cups. Using cling wrap, mold more rice into round balls for the panda's ears and oval balls for its legs and tail.

3. Cut out a piece of nori large enough to wrap around the rice balls that form the ears, legs, and tail. Make cuts at the corners.

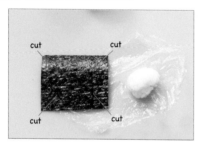

4. Place rice on nori.

5. Wrap into a ball with cling wrap and set aside for the nori to mold nicely onto the rice. Repeat for the rest of the ears, legs, and tail.

6. Fold nori in half and cut out panda's eyes, using a pair of scissors.

7. Using a pair of scissors, cut out panda's nose.

8. Using a pair of tweezers, place nori cutouts onto the panda's face.

9. Line bento box with lettuce and place panda inside. Attach on the ears, limbs, and tail using pasta sticks.

10. Cut ovals from carrots using a cutter to form the panda's cheeks. Secure onto rice balls using pasta sticks.

11. Use food cups, lettuce, or wax paper to separate food in the bento box. Arrange the rest of the food in the bento box and pack tightly so the food will not shift when it is being transported.

12. Cut carrots into slices approximately 0.5cm thick. Use a flower cutter to cut out carrots.

13. Cut lines from the center of the flowers to the edge of the petals. Cut about halfway down, but not all the way through.

14. Place the knife in the middle of one petal and make a slanted 45-degree cut to the left of the petal.

15. This is how it looks after cutting.

16. You can boil the carrots if you prefer.

Ice Cream Buddies

Yes, you can pack ice cream in your bento box—just make them out of rice! This double scoop of bunny and chick ice cream will definitely not melt before lunchtime. For side dishes, shape meat patties on ice cream sticks to complete the ice cream theme. The cone is made from aburaage, which are thin slices of deep-fried tofu.

BENTO MENU	FOOD ART INGREDIENTS	TOOLS NEEDED
Cajun spiced grilled wings (p. 208)	Rice	Cling wrap
Pork carrot patties (p. 216)	Hard-boiled egg yolk	Tweezers
Tamagoyaki (p. 225)	Sakura denbu/pink sushi mix	Hole punch
Lettuce	Nori	Craft punch
Strawberries	Carrot	Round cutter/straw
Grapes	Aburaage	Knife
		Strawberry bento picks

1. Mix a portion of rice with sakura denbu or pink sushi mix to make it pink. Using cling wrap, shape the bunny's head and ears. The head should look like a dome.

2. Mix another portion of rice with mashed hard-boiled egg yolk for the chick.

3. Using cling wrap, shape the yellow rice into a dome shape for the chick's head.

4. Using cling wrap, shape the remaining plain white rice into a cone shape. Wrap a sheet of aburaage around the rice. Wrap again in cling wrap to secure.

5. Cut strips of aburaage and arrange it in a criss-cross manner around the cone. Secure with pasta sticks.

6. Use hole punch and craft punch to punch out the eyes and mouths from a nori sheet for the bunny and chick.

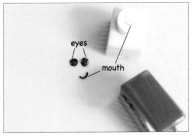

7. Cut out an oval from the carrot using a cutter to make the beak.

8. Assemble the different parts in the bento box. Punch out ovals from ham using a cutter to form the cheeks.

Baby Bear

Shhh…don't disturb the sleeping baby bear! Make this huggable baby bear out of rice mixed with a little dark soy sauce—dark soy sauce is thicker than and not as salty as light soy sauce, so it will provide a nice brown color without altering the taste of the rice too much.

BENTO MENU

Chicken nuggets (p. 203)
Butter mushrooms (p. 230)
Sesame broccoli (p. 227)
Corn
Lettuce

FOOD ART INGREDIENTS

Rice
Dark soy sauce/teriyaki
  sauce
Nori
Black olives
Ham
Cherry tomato
Pasta sticks

TOOLS NEEDED

Cling wrap
Tweezers
Scissors
Nori punch
Paw craft punch
Round cutter/straw
Leaf bento pick
Musical note bento pick

1. Add a little dark soy sauce or teriyaki sauce to warm rice. Add a few drops at a time until you get your desired shade. Mix well until the color is even.

2. Using cling wrap, shape the bear's head, body, ears, hands, and legs.

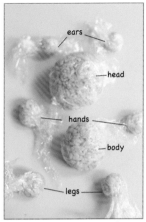

3. Line a bento box with lettuce and assemble the bear in the box, filling up the gaps with broccoli. Use pasta to secure the ears, hands, and legs to the main body of the bear.

4. Punch out eyes from a nori sheet using a nori punch. Cut out the nose from an olive using a pair of scissors.

5. Use a paw craft punch to cut out paw cutouts from the nori. Use a round cutter to cut out ovals in the ham for the bear's cheeks.

6. Attach a leaf bento pick onto a cherry tomato for a final touch.

Bunny and Sunflower

A playful bunny plays among the sunflowers with his ladybug friend. You can make these lovely sunflowers using sausages and egg sheets. The tiny apple in this bento is made from cherry tomato and washi tape—a colorful, decorative tape for crafters—that is stuck on a toothpick. You can also use washi tape to make little flags to decorate your bento box. The side dish for this bento is chicken tofu patties, which are soft and juicy.

BENTO MENU	FOOD ART INGREDIENTS	TOOLS NEEDED
Chicken tofu patties (p. 210)	Rice	Cling wrap
Sesame broccoli (p. 227)	Sausage	Tweezers
Cherry tomato	Egg sheet	Knife
Lettuce	Nori	Nori punch
	Pasta sticks	Oval cutter/straw
	Ham	Green washi tape
		Toothpick
		Ladybug bento pick
		Donut bento pick

1. Using cling wrap, shape rice into a rice ball for the bunny's head. Using cling wrap, shape the bunny's ears and hands.

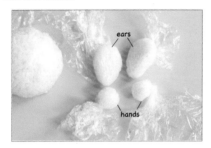

2. Use a nori punch to cut out the bunny's eyes and nose from a sheet of nori. Using scissors, cut out a straight line from nori for the mouth.

3. Use an oval cutter to cut the ham to make the bunny's cheeks.

4. Assemble bunny in the bento box. Use pasta sticks to attach the ears.

5. Make crisscross cuts in the cross-section of the sausages. Boil the sausages—the crisscross cut pattern will become obvious after it's cooked.

6. Fold egg sheet in half and make cuts along the folded edge in intervals of around ¼ inch.

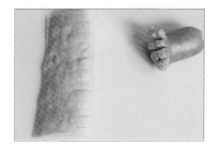

7. Wrap the egg sheet around the sausage cross-section and secure the ends using pasta sticks.

8. To make the apple, make a flag on a toothpick using washi tape. Trim the tape into a leaf shape and poke it through a cherry tomato.

Penguin Onigiri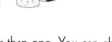

Pack a pair of chubby penguins in a little bento, because two is cuter than one. You can choose to shape the rice balls bigger or smaller, according to your little one's appetite. Most kids love ketchup, so the ketchup shrimp in this side dish will certainly stimulate their appetite.

BENTO MENU

Ketchup shrimp (p. 219)
Cajun spiced grilled
    wings (p. 208)
Sesame broccoli (p. 227)
Lettuce

FOOD ART INGREDIENTS

Rice
Nori
Carrot
Corn
Pasta sticks

TOOLS NEEDED

Cling wrap
Tweezers
Scissors
Nori punch
Round cutter/straw
Knife

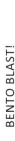

1. Scoop rice onto cling wrap, twist ends, and shape it into an oval rice ball. Check to see if it fits your bento box. Add or remove more rice if needed.

2. Fold a sheet of nori in half and cut out the shape according to the photo below.

3. Open up the nori sheet.

4. Place the nori on the rice ball and wrap with cling wrap to secure it.

5. Use a nori punch to cut out the eyes.

6. Use a pasta stick to attach a piece of corn onto the rice ball for the penguin's beak.

7. Use a round cutter to cut out circles from the carrot. Attach onto the rice ball using pasta sticks.

8. Assemble the penguins in the bento box, using lettuce and broccoli to separate and fill out the gaps.

Baby Pandas

Roly poly baby pandas play in a bamboo grove. They are so adorable that it's difficult not to pop them in your mouth! One of the side dishes in this bento is lemon soy sauce salmon, a fish that is rich in omega 3. The salmon is first pan-fried until crisp before it is drizzled over with a refreshing lemon soy sauce dressing.

BENTO MENU

Lemon soy sauce salmon
  (p. 222)
Crispy chicken fillet (p. 215)
Green beans and mushroom
  stir-fry (p. 229)

FOOD ART INGREDIENTS

Rice
Nori
Green beans

TOOLS NEEDED

Cling wrap
Tweezers
Scissors
Knife
Panda nori punch

1. Using cling wrap, shape rice into a ball. Repeat and make another one or two rice balls. Cut out a wide strip of nori and place on the rice ball. Wrap with cling wrap to secure.

2. Cut out panda's eyes, ears, nose, and tail from a sheet of nori using a nori punch.

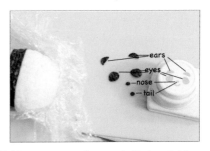

3. Use tweezers to place the nori cutouts onto the rice.

4. Fold a new nori sheet in half, then fold it in half again. Cut out panda legs using a pair of scissors.

5. Place the panda's legs onto the rice ball. Wrap with cling wrap to secure. Cut out the panda's ears, eyes, and nose from the nori using a nori punch and place on the rice ball.

6. Blanch the green beans. Make slanted slits on the bean using a knife. Repeat on another one.

7. Slice another green bean into slanted cuts.

8. Assemble the green beans in your bento box.

Puffer Fish

We won't be able to pack real poisonous puffer fish, also known as fugu, in our bento since we aren't trained to remove its toxins! However, we can craft a puffer fish that is safe for our children to eat out of rice and nori instead. This bento is packed with pork stir-fried with cabbage, a quick dish to whip up for lunch.

BENTO MENU
Pork cabbage stir-fry
  (p. 216)
Tamagoyaki (p. 225)
Lettuce
Cherry tomato
Edamame

FOOD ART INGREDIENTS
Rice
Ham
Cheese
Nori

TOOLS NEEDED
Cling wrap
Tweezers
Scissors
Round cutters
Hole punch
Sea creatures bento picks

1. Shape the rice ball using cling wrap. Cut out a piece of nori to wrap around the top portion of the rice ball. Make some cuts at the top so it will be easier to fold.

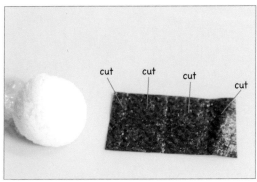

2. Wrap nori around the top half of rice ball. Wrap with cling wrap to secure and set aside.

3. Using a round cutter, cut out two circles from a slice of cheese for the eyes. Use a large round cutter to cut out a circle of ham, then use a smaller round cutter to make a second round cut inside the circle to form a ring on the outside.

4. Use a pair of scissors to cut out triangles from a sheet of nori. Use a hole punch to cut out circles from the nori.

5. Assemble the parts onto the rice ball using a pair of tweezers.

Soboro Lion

Soboro is a delicious, savory topping, usually as an accompaniment to plain rice, that is made using ground meat. Any kind of ground meat can be used—beef, pork, veal, or turkey, for example. In addition to a topping, soboro can also be used as an onigiri filling. You can prepare a larger quantity of soboro and store it in the fridge for up to a week or freeze to keep it longer. In this bento, I've used soboro to create the mane of a lion.

BENTO MENU

Honey chicken (p. 214)

Grilled mushrooms

Broccoli and carrot
   stir-fry (p. 230)

Soy sauce okra (p. 230)

FOOD ART INGREDIENTS

Rice

Meat soboro (p. 215)

Nori

Black olives

Black sesame seeds

Fried pasta

TOOLS NEEDED

Cling wrap

Tweezers

Scissors

1. Fill a round bento box with rice and use cling wrap to press the rice down lightly.

2. Add a layer of soboro as an outer ring around the rice.

3. Cut out the lion's nose from olives. Cut out the lion's eyes and mouth from a sheet of nori.

4. Using tweezers, place black sesame seeds.

5. Add fried pasta for the lion's whiskers.

Scrambled Eggs Clown

In this bento, scrambled egg forms the clown's hair, while a little cherry tomato is perfect for the clown's red nose. A lovely piece of farfalle pasta, also known as bow-tie pasta, adds the final touch as the clown's bow.

BENTO MENU

Honey chicken (p. 214)
Ground pork and potato
   stir-fry (p. 211)
Blanched broccoli

FOOD ART INGREDIENTS

Rice
Scrambled eggs
Nori
Cherry tomato
Farfalle pasta
Pasta sticks

TOOLS NEEDED

Cling wrap
Tweezers
Scissors

1. Fill a round bento box with rice. Use cling wrap to press the rice down lightly.

2. Add a layer of scrambled eggs on the top portion of the bento to form the clown's hair.

3. Use a cherry tomato as the clown's nose and attach it onto the rice using pasta sticks if needed. Use a pair of scissors to cut out nori for the clown's features.

4. Add a piece of farfalle pasta for the clown's bow.

Ninjas

The boys will be thrilled to bring this cool ninja bento box to school, and even the girls would love these cute-looking ninjas! Nori is the perfect ingredient to make the ninja's outfit. Sakura denbu, a pinkish fluffy flaked fish condiment usually used in sushi rolls, is used to flush the ninja's cheeks. Sakura denbu can be bought in packets in Japanese supermarkets or online; otherwise a suitable substitute would be to use pink cake decorating gel.

BENTO MENU

Lemon soy sauce salmon
    (p. 222)
Lemon chicken (p. 212)
Broccoli and carrot
    stir-fry (p. 230)
Tamagoyaki (p. 225)
Apples
Carrots

FOOD ART INGREDIENTS

Rice
Nori
Cheese
Sakura denbu/ketchup

TOOLS NEEDED

Cling wrap
Knife
Scissors
Tweezers
Toothpick
Nori punch

1. Using cling wrap, shape two rice balls for the head and body. For the body, use your hand to continue molding the rice ball into an inverted "V." Using cling wrap, shape more rice into two long cylindrical shapes for the hands.

2. Wrap all body parts with nori (note that you won't be wrapping the underside of the rice balls). Starting with the head, cut nori into two shapes as shown, then make cuts along the lines to make it easier to wrap. Place nori on the rice ball and use cling wrap to secure and shape.

3. To wrap the arms, cut nori roughly as shown in the picture, then make rough cuts along the lines. Place nori on the rice ball that is your ninja's arm and use cling wrap to wrap, secure, and shape.

4. To wrap the body, cut nori roughly as shown in the picture, then make rough cuts along the lines. Place nori on the rice ball that is your ninja's body and use cling wrap to wrap, secure, and shape.

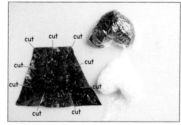

5. Cut out a heart-shaped scarf for the ninja from a sheet of nori using a pair of scissors. Place the nori on a slice of cheese and cut out using a toothpick.

6. For the sword, cut out a small rectangle of cheese, then cut out small strips of nori to wrap around it.

7. Use a nori punch to cut out the eyes from nori. Cut a curved line for the nose using scissors. Dab on sakura denbu or ketchup for the cheeks.

8. Assemble all the parts on a plate or in a bento box.

Baby Inari Sushi

Have a newborn in the family? Celebrate the birth by packing a bento with a pair of babies sleeping in cribs, complete with egg blankets. Learn to prepare salted salmon, which can be prepared in advance in a large batch, kept frozen, and thawed and grilled when required. This helps to save the preparation time.

BENTO MENU

Ketchup shrimp (p. 219)
Salted salmon (p. 222)
Broccoli and carrot stir-fry
    (p. 230)
Corn
Purple potatoes
Cherry tomato

FOOD ART INGREDIENTS

Aburaage
Rice
Egg sheet
Ketchup

TOOLS NEEDED

Cling wrap
Tweezers
Craft punch
Nori punch
Star cutter
Chopstick

1. Color rice a pale pink with ketchup. Using cling wrap, shape rice into two small balls. Open up an aburaage pouch and stuff it with the two rice balls.

2. Make an egg sheet (p. 14). Slice into a rectangle and use it to cover the bottom rice ball like a blanket.

3. Use nori and craft punchers to cut out the babies' features from a sheet of nori.

4. Use a chopstick to dot on some ketchup for their cheeks.

5. Use a star cutter to cut out boiled purple potatoes.

Witch

Kids are always fascinated by magical witches and wizards. Pack this friendly looking witch onigiri in their bentos. Craft her hair out of fusilli pasta, and make her a broomstick out of ham and pretzel sticks. Have a picky kid who hates carrots? Then use carrots to make delicious pork carrot patties as a side dish.

BENTO MENU

Pork carrot patties (p. 216)
Tamagoyaki (p. 225)
Sesame broccoli (p. 227)
Cherry tomatoes
Purple potatoes
Lettuce

FOOD ART INGREDIENTS

Rice
Ketchup
Ham
Nori
Fusilli
Pasta stick
Pretzel sticks

TOOLS NEEDED

Cling wrap
Tweezers
Scissors
Nori punch
Witch's hat cupcake topper
Round cutter

1. Color rice balls by mixing with ketchup. Using cling wrap, shape out two rice balls—a bigger one for the head and a smaller one for the body.

2. Using a nori punch, cut out ovals for the eyes from a sheet of nori. Using a pair of scissors, cut out a curved thin line for the mouth.

3. Cut a sheet of nori bigger than the triangular rice ball. Then, cut along the four edges as shown.

4. Wrap nori around the rice ball and shape with cling wrap. Set aside.

5. For the broomstick, you need a pretzel stick and a small slice of ham. Fold ham in half and make regular parallel cuts along the edge. Don't cut all the way through—just about three-quarters in.

6. Wrap ham around the end of the pretzel stick and secure in place with a pasta stick.

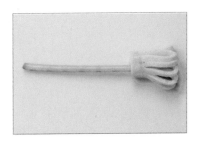

7. Assemble rice balls in the bento box. Add fusilli pasta for her hair and add a witch's hat cupcake topper.

8. Using a round cutter, cut out two small circles from the ham for her cheeks. Use pasta sticks to secure them onto the rice ball.

Sleeping Kitty Cat

Mummy cat and baby kitty snuggle under a polka-dotted egg blanket. Learn to make the polka-dotted egg blanket from the step-by-step pictures below. This same idea can also be used in a sandwich—simply use a slice of bread to fold over the cats instead. This bento is packed with a cheesy fish fillet, a fillet coated in an egg and Parmesan mixture and pan-fried until crispy, which kids just love.

BENTO MENU
Cheesy fish fillet (p. 221)
Broccoli and carrot stir-fry
   (p. 230)
Strawberries

FOOD ART INGREDIENTS
Chicken egg
Quail egg
Nori
Egg yolk (separated)
Egg white (separated)
Pasta sticks
Cake decorating gel

TOOLS NEEDED
Knife
Tweezers
Scissors
Paw craft punch
Tamagoyaki pan
Chopstick
Round cutter

1. Use egg yolk to make a yellow egg sheet (p. 14). Place the egg sheet on a cutting mat. Use a round cutter or the back of your piping tip to cut circles in the egg sheet. These circles form the polka dots.

2. Return the egg sheet to the pan, turn on the stove to low heat, and pour the egg whites into the holes. Cook until the egg whites have set. Set aside the egg sheet.

3. Prepare a hard-boiled chicken egg. Slice the egg in half. Keep half of the egg for the mother cat's head. Using a knife or a pair of scissors, cut out the cat's ears and hand from the other half of the hard-boiled egg.

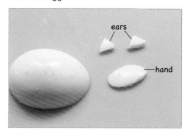

4. Using a paw craft punch, cut an oval for the mother cat's nose from nori. Using scissors, cut two curved lines and six short lines from the nori for the cat's eyes and whiskers.

5. Prepare a hard-boiled quail egg and repeat the same steps as above to form the baby kitty. However, you do not need to cut out the kitty's hand.

6. Dab cake decorating gel on both the chicken and quail eggs for the cheeks. Assemble the eggs on the rice and cover with the egg blanket. Use pasta sticks to secure if needed.

7. Alternatively, you can also cut out a slice of bread and fold it over the egg; secure using pasta sticks.

8. These sleeping kitty sandwiches can also be packed in a bento box.

Hot Dog Bear Sushi

Maki sushi, one of the most common types of sushi that consists of a rice rolled in nori, is an easy lunchtime meal for the little ones to hold and eat as they can usually be consumed in one mouthful. This sushi roll uses hot dogs as a filling instead of traditional Japanese maki fillings such as seafood or vegetables. Additionally, if your child has developed a mature love for spicy food, you can learn to make a spicy side dish of stir-fried asparagus with sriracha chili sauce. Alternatively, you can substitute this spicy asparagus side with asparagus and corn stir-fry (p. 231) for a milder kid-friendly version.

BENTO MENU	FOOD ART INGREDIENTS	TOOLS NEEDED
Grilled chicken balls (p. 208)	Rice	Sushi mat
Sriracha asparagus (p. 228)	Sausages	Knife
Squash stir-fry (p. 228)	Cheese	Tweezers
Red currants	Nori	Round cutter/straw
Lettuce	Ketchup	Paw craft punch
		Chopstick

1. Place a sheet of nori on a bamboo mat and spread rice on top. Place a hot dog in the middle.

2. Roll the sushi rice over the sausage with the help of a sushi bamboo mat.

3. Wet knife with damp towel before slicing the sushi.

4. Using a round cutter, cut out three circles from a slice of cheese for the bear's ears and snout.

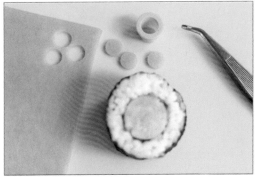

5. Use a craft punch to cut out shapes in a sheet of nori for the bear's eyes and mouth. Using a chopstick, dab on ketchup for the cheeks.

Scrambled Eggs Chick

Scrambled eggs, which are perfect for breakfast, make a yummy addition to your lunchtime bento menu. Shape your scrambled eggs into a little chick to decorate your box. This bento menu also contains seaweed pork rolls. Thinly sliced pork is wrapped with nori and rolled up tightly. The rolls are then coated in panko, Japanese-style bread crumbs. If you can't get hold of panko, substitute normal bread crumbs.

BENTO MENU

Rice
Seaweed pork rolls (p. 202)
Ketchup shrimp (p. 219)
Sesame broccoli (p. 227)
Carrots
Lettuce

FOOD ART INGREDIENTS

Scrambled eggs (p. 224)
Nori
Carrot
Ketchup

TOOLS NEEDED

Cling wrap
Scissors
Tweezers
Nori punch
Chopstick

1. Scoop scrambled eggs onto a sheet of cling wrap.

2. Wrap cling wrap around scrambled eggs to shape the chick's body. Repeat and shape the chick's wings.

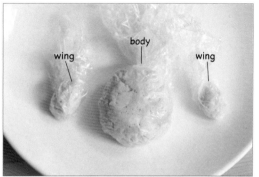

3. Using an oval-shaped cutter or a straw squeezed into an oval shape with your fingers, cut out an oval from a slice of carrot. This will be the chick's beak.

4. Using a nori punch, cut out the chick's eyes and feet from a sheet of nori.

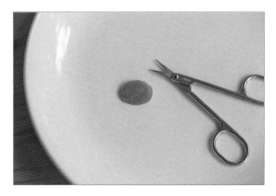

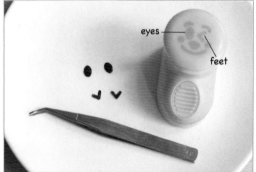

5. Assemble the beak, eyes, and feet of the chick using a pair of tweezers. Dab on some ketchup using a chopstick for its cheeks.

Tomato Ladybugs

Dainty ladybugs rest among four-leaf clovers. These edible ladybugs are made from tomatoes and the four-leaf clovers from cucumbers. The side dish for this bento is lemon chicken, a tangy, sweet, and savory dish. Chicken is fried until crispy, then coated in a refreshing citrus lemon sauce.

BENTO MENU	FOOD ART INGREDIENTS	TOOLS NEEDED
Rice	Cherry tomatoes	Cling wrap
Lemon chicken (p. 212)	Nori	Knife
Broccoli	Sesame seeds	Tweezers
Lettuce	Cucumber	Hole punch
Bell peppers	Pasta sticks	Heart-shaped cutter
	Mayonnaise	Ramekin

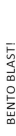

1. Wrap rice in cling wrap and fit into a small ramekin to help shape it round.

2. Cut out a strip of nori and wrap it around the circumference of the rice ball.

3. Slice cherry tomato in half.

4. Cut out a semi-circle about half the size of the cherry tomato and a long strip from a sheet of nori using a pair of scissors. Cut out smaller circles from the nori using a hole punch.

5. Dab on some mayonnaise on the tomato as "glue" and arrange the nori cutouts as shown in the picture. Wrap with cling wrap for the nori to adhere to the tomato.

6. Use a heart-shaped cutter to make cutouts in a cucumber.

7. Assemble the various parts on the rice, use pasta sticks to secure, and add sesame seeds for the ladybug's trail. Cut a long strip of cucumber to form the stalk of the leaf clover.

Piggy Spam Musubi

Spam musubi is a popular snack and lunchtime meal in Hawaii that comes from both Japanese and American influences. It consists of a slice of grilled Spam on top of a block of rice, wrapped together with nori. This simple creation hits an extremely high point on the scale of tastiness, and will certainly be a hit with most children. In this bento, I will take you though the steps on how to make Spam musubi and craft them into a pair of piggies.

BENTO MENU

Veggie pork/beef rolls
    (p. 206)
Broccoli and carrot stir-fry
    (p. 230)
Corn
Cherry tomato
Lettuce

FOOD ART INGREDIENTS

Rice
Spam
Ham
Nori
Pasta sticks

TOOLS NEEDED

Spam tin
Cling wrap
Scissors
Tweezers
Oval cutters
Nori punch

1. Cut two slices of Spam. Add a little oil to a pan and panfry Spam until lightly browned on both sides.

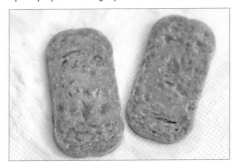

2. Line the Spam tin with cling wrap. Scoop rice into the tin.

3. Cover the rice with cling wrap and use your hands to compress the rice together.

4. Pull out the cling wrap and remove the rice.

5. Place a slice of Spam on the rice. Cut out a strip of nori and wrap it around the Spam-and-rice sandwich.

6. Using a knife or a pair of scissors, cut out an oval from a slice of ham for the pig's snout. Using an oval cutter, cut out six smaller ovals for the pig's ears and feet. Cut out an inverted "V" at the edges of four of the ovals to form the cloven hooves.

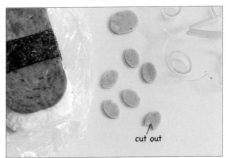

cut out

7. Use pasta sticks to secure the ham onto the Spam. Use a nori punch to cut out piggy's eyes and nostrils from a nori sheet.

eyes

snout

Koala Onigiri

Deco-furi is a fast and convenient way to color your rice. If you have no access to deco-furi, you can use purple carrots or potatoes to dye your rice purple (p. 10). Learn to make a bow out of ham, a great addition to any girl-themed bentos for your daughters.

BENTO MENU

Salted salmon (p. 222)

Green beans and
    mushroom stir-fry
    (p. 229)

Corn

Lettuce

Strawberries

FOOD ART INGREDIENTS

Rice

Deco-furi

Ham

Nori

Pasta sticks

TOOLS NEEDED

Cling wrap

Tweezers

Scissors

Hole punch

Oval cutter/straw

Koala bento pick

1. Mix purple deco-furi with warm rice.

2. Mix until rice is evenly colored.

3. Using cling wrap, shape the koala's head, ears, and hands.

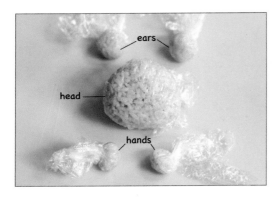

4. Using a hole punch, cut out circles from a sheet of nori. Cut out the koala's nose from the nori using a pair of scissors.

5. Cut the ham using an oval cutter to form the koala's cheeks.

6. Cut out a circle and a strip from the ham.

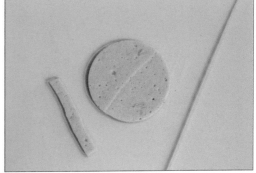

7. Shape the circle into a bow and use the strip of ham to wrap it round the the middle.

8. Secure the bow with a pasta stick.

9. Take the koala's ears and flatten them by pressing them in the middle.

10. Assemble the ears onto the koala onigiri. You can use pasta sticks to secure them to prevent them from moving.

Bento and Food Art Tutorials

BREAD-BASED BENTOS

Bear Sandwich Rolls

Add a twist to your usual packed sandwiches by rolling them up instead. This makes it easier for little fingers to hold and eat the pieces of bread. During preparation, instead of discarding the bread crusts, use them to transform your sandwich rolls into an adorable pair of bears.

BENTO MENU	FOOD ART INGREDIENTS	TOOLS NEEDED
Kiwis	Bread	Cling wrap
Strawberries	Cheese	Knife
Blueberries	Ham	Tweezers
Lettuce	Nori	Round cutter/piping tip
	Pasta sticks	Oval cutter/straw
		Nori punch

1. Slice off bread crusts. Flatten bread using a rolling pin. This helps to prevent the bread from breaking apart when they are later rolled up.

2. Butter the bread and add a slice of cheese and ham. Slowly roll up the bread.

3. Wrap the rolled up sandwich in cling wrap and set aside for 5 minutes.

4. Remove cling wrap and slice off the edges if needed so that the sandwich can fit into your bento box.

5. Cut out circles from bread crusts using a round cutter or the back of a piping tip. These will form the bears' ears and snout.

6. Attach the ears and snout using pasta sticks.

7. Using a nori punch, make cutouts in a sheet of nori to make the bears' eyes, noses, and mouths.

8. Squeeze your straw into an oval shape and use it to cut out ovals from a slice of ham to form the cheeks. Attach onto the sandwich roll using pasta sticks.

Penguin Sandwich

This penguin sandwich is made using white and mulit-grained bread, two types of bread with different colors and textures that will easily form the two-toned body of a penguin. Pack this in a penguin-themed bento box to complete the look and add snowflakes cut out from cucumbers as a final touch.

BENTO MENU

Cajun spiced grilled
  wings (p. 208)
Grapes
Strawberries

FOOD ART INGREDIENTS

Brown bread
White bread
Peanut butter
Carrots
Blueberries
Cheese
Cucumbers
Pasta sticks

TOOLS NEEDED

Circle-shaped cutters
Oval-shaped cutter
Snowflake cutter
Knife

1. Use a round bento box to make round cutouts on two slices of bread—one brown and one white.

2. Make a smaller circular cutout inside the round piece of brown bread using a small round cutter. Use the same round cutter to cut out a circle from the round piece of white bread. This should give you two small round slices of white and brown bread and two large slices of white and brown bread with a circular cutout in their centers.

3. Assemble in the bento box. Slip the smaller circle of brown bread into the empty cutout in the slice of white bread to form the bottom layer of the sandwich. Do the opposite for the top layer of the sandwich by slipping the smaller circle of white bread into the empty cutout in the slice of brown bread. Spread peanut butter on the bottom layer, and sandwich. Cut out the penguin's eyes from cheese using a small round cutter and place a blueberry on top of each for the pupils. Secure in place using pasta sticks.

4. Use an oval cutter to cut out the penguin's beak and feet from a slice of carrot. Secure on the penguin's sandwich body using pasta sticks.

5. Use a snowflake-shaped cutter to make cutouts in a cucumber slice.

Piggy Pocket Sandwich

Don't own a pocket sandwich mold? Don't worry; you don't need one to make a pocket sandwich! Pocket sandwiches are sealed at the edges so the fillings do not fall out, making it easier for your little ones to hold them. You can make a pocket sandwich using any bowl or cup in your kitchen. Add some ham and nori and transform your sandwiches into cute little piggies to adorn your bento.

BENTO MENU	FOOD ART INGREDIENTS	TOOLS NEEDED
Bell peppers	White bread	Bowl
Potato salad (p. 228)	Ham	Scissors
Grapes	Nori	Straw/round cutter
	Cheese	Tweezers
	Mayonnaise	

1. Using a bowl, make a light imprint on a slice of bread.

2. Place your ingredients on the inside of the circular outline of the imprint.

3. Place a slice of bread over the top to form the sandwich. Using a bowl, press down hard on the sandwich and rock to and fro until the sandwich is cut through.

4. The sandwich will be sealed after it is cut through.

5. Cut out the pig's ears and snout from a slice of ham using a pair of scissors.

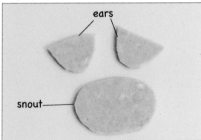

6. Use a straw to cut out two circles from the snout.

7. Spread mayonnaise on the ham cutouts and place the pig's ears and snout on the sandwich. Using scissors, cut out the pig's eyes from nori. You can cut ovals for opened eyes and curved lines for closed eyes to vary their expressions.

8. Spread mayonnaise on the nori cutouts and place on the sandwich using a pair of tweezers. Use a straw to cut out two circles from cheese to form the cheeks and place on the sandwich.

Snail Sandwich

The snails in this bento are made from a heart-shaped pocket sandwich. Learn to make this pocket sandwich using two heart-shaped cutters, one slightly larger than the other. Eye bento picks come in handy and will save you the trouble of making the snail's eyes from scratch. This bento tutorial also includes instructions to craft a mock sliced apple using a cherry tomato.

BENTO MENU

Apples

Cherry tomatoes

Carrots

Lettuce

FOOD ART INGREDIENTS

White bread

Peanut butter

Dark colored cheese

Light colored cheese

Cherry tomatoes

Cucumber

Black sesame seeds

Mayonnaise

TOOLS NEEDED

Heart-shaped cutters

Round cutters

Eye bento picks

Nori punch

Tweezers

Knife

1. You need two heart-shaped cutters, one larger than the other. Cut out two hearts in bread using the bigger cutter. Spread peanut butter in the middle but don't overfill it.

2. Use the blunt edge of the smaller cutter and press hard against the bread to seal the edges together.

3. Remove the cutter and you have a heart-shaped pocket sandwich.

4. Cut out circles from cheese using three circle cutters of different sizes.

5. Place cheese cutouts on sandwich. Poke eye food picks into the sandwich as shown to form the snail's shell.

6. Using a nori punch, cut out the mouth from a sheet of nori. Dab some mayonnaise on the nori cutout before using a pair of tweezers to place the nori on the snail sandwich.

7. To make tomato apples, slice a cherry tomato in half. Using a round cutter or the back of a piping tip, make a circle cutout in a slice of cheese. The cutout should be smaller than the cherry tomato. Cut the cheese in half.

8. Place black sesame seeds on the cheese as shown. To form the apple stem, make a cutout in a slice of cucumber as shown. Use a knife to make a small slit in the top of the cherry tomato and insert the stem.

Mashed Potato Duck Sandwich 🍞

Does your little one love bath time with his favorite rubber ducky? Learn to make little ducks for his or her lunchtime bento using mashed potatoes. Mashed potatoes are similar to Play-Doh as they can be molded into lots of different characters—the only limit is your imagination. The sandwiches, salad, and mashed potatoes for this bento can be prepared the day before and kept in the fridge, so you won't have to rush to get the food ready in the morning.

BENTO MENU

Ham and lettuce
    sandwich
Broccoli pasta salad

FOOD ART INGREDIENTS

Mashed potatoes (p. 177,
    steps 1 and 2)
Nori
Yellow gel food coloring/
    hard-boiled egg yolk
Orange gel food coloring/
    steamed mashed squash

TOOLS NEEDED

Cling wrap
Hole punch
Tweezers

1. Prepare mashed potatoes. Add yellow gel-based food coloring to the mashed potatoes. To color mashed potato yellow naturally, mix in hard-boiled egg yolks.

2. Scoop out 1 tbsp of mashed potatoes and add some orange gel-based food coloring. To color orange naturally, mix in steamed mashed squash.

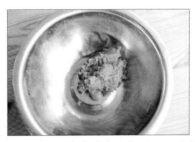

3. To make the duck, roll yellow mashed potato into two balls, one slightly bigger than the other.

4. Take the bigger ball, flatten the front a little, and shape out a little pointy tip at the back to create the duck's tail.

5. Place the smaller ball on top of the body. Take orange-colored mashed potato, shape out the duck's bill, and mold it onto the duck.

6. Punch out a circle from a sheet of nori using a hole punch for the eye.

7. You can either stop here or continue by taking some yellow mashed potato and shaping the duck's wings as shown.

Animal Bread Balls

Bread balls are pieces of bread that have been stuffed with fillings and shaped into a ball, making it more fun for little ones to eat. Style your bread balls into a set of adorable animals for your child to bring to school. They can be filled with traditional sandwich fillings such as egg salad, tuna salad, ham, cheese, or jam.

BENTO MENU

Canned tuna
Pork nuggets (p. 205)
Red currants
Lettuce
Bell pepper stir-fry

FOOD ART INGREDIENTS

White bread
Multi-grained bread
Canned tuna
Mayonnaise
Pea
Blueberries
Nori
Ketchup
Pasta sticks

TOOLS NEEDED

Cling wrap
Rolling pin
Scissors
Nori punch
Knife
Round cutter/piping tip
Chopstick

1. Slice off the bread crust and set aside. Roll the bread flat using a rolling pin. Make cuts in the middle of the four edges of the bread as shown.

2. Drain off liquid from canned tuna. In a bowl, mix it with 4 tbsp mayonnaise. Add a pinch of salt and black pepper. Spread tuna salad in the center of the bread but do not put too much.

3. Bring the four corners together and wrap and secure the bread using cling wrap. Twist the ends tight and shape into a ball. Leave aside for a while.

4. Place bread balls in baking cups. For my bento, I used both white and mutligrained breads to get a variety of color for my animals.

5. To make a bunny, cut out a circle from a piece of bread using the back of a piping tip.

6. Place a pea on a pasta stick and use it to secure the circular bread cutout onto the bread ball to form the bunny's nose.

7. With a pair of scissors, cut out the bunny's ears from a piece of bread. Cut two slits in the bread ball using a knife so you can slot in the ears.

8. Use a nori punch to cut out the bunny's eyes from a sheet of nori. Cut out a straight line from the nori using scissors. Dab on some mayonnaise before using tweezers to place the nori cutouts on the bread ball.

eyes

9. Dab on ketchup using a chopstick for the bunny's cheeks.

10. To make a bear, use the same methods to create the bear's facial features as the bunny bread ball. Cut out ears from the leftover bread crust using a round cutter. Attach the ears to the bread ball using pasta sticks.

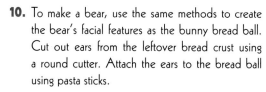

11. To make a dog, use the same methods to create the dog's facial features as the bunny bread ball. Cut out the ears from bread crust using a pair of scissors. Attach the ears to the bread ball using pasta sticks.

12. To make a panda, use the same methods to create the panda's facial features as the bunny bread ball. However, its eyes should be made from a larger nori oval cutout, as shown, and a blueberry will form its nose instead of a pea. Blueberries form the panda's ears and should be secured to the bread ball using pasta sticks.

13. Here are the four completed animal bread balls.

Chicks in Bread Cup Nests 🍞

Bread cups are a creative way to arrange and serve your sandwiches. Kids will love this fun way of eating. In this bento, bread is first cut and toasted, filled with toppings and cheese, then returned to the oven to toast until the cheese melts. Decorate these bread cup nests with a pair of hens made using quail eggs.

BENTO MENU	FOOD ART INGREDIENTS	TOOLS NEEDED
Bread	Quail eggs	Round cutters
Tuna salad (p. 79, step 2)	Corn	Scissors
Mozzarella	Pasta sticks	Aluminum foil cups/
Grapes	Nori	ramekin
Strawberries	Pink cake decorating gel	Heart-shaped bento pick
	Mayonnaise	Paw craft punch
		Tweezers

1. Prepare two round cutters, one smaller and the other larger.

2. The larger cutter should be slightly smaller than the base of the aluminum baking cup that you will be using.

3. Use the blunt side of the cutter, instead of the sharp cutting side, to make an imprint in the middle of the bread.

4. Use the smaller cutter to make imprints along the edge of the big circle imprint as shown, so it looks like a flower with petals.

5. Use a pair of scissors to cut out the bread, following along the imprinted outline. This will give you a five-petal bread cup.

6. Place the bread into the aluminum baking cup as shown. Bake the bread at around 350°F (180°C) for 8 minutes in the oven.

7. Alternatively, you can also use the big cutter to make all the imprints instead. This gives you a four-petal bread cup.

8. Similarly, use a pair of scissors to cut out the bread, following the imprinted outline.

9. Place the bread into the aluminum baking cup. Bake the bread at around 350°F (180°C) for 8 minutes in the oven.

10. Take the cups out and fill them with whatever you want to stuff the bread with, such as tuna salad.

11. Top with cheese and return to the oven to bake until the cheese melts.

12. Remove from oven and allow to cool.

13. Prepare and peel hard-boiled quail eggs. Use a craft punch to cut out two ovals in nori for the eyes. Dab on mayonnaise as "glue" to stick them on the egg. Use a pasta stick to attach corn to the egg for the hen's beak.

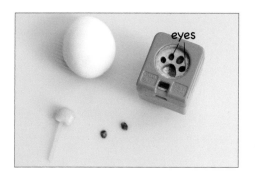

14. Add a heart-shaped bento pick for the hen's comb. Dab on some pink decorating gel for the hen's cheeks.

Hot Dog Bunnies 🍞

A trio of playful bunnies play peek-a-boo among a garden of sandwich rolls. These sandwich rolls are made from a mix of chicken salad and hot dog fillings.

BENTO MENU

Chicken salad (p. 209)
Potato salad (p. 228)
Lettuce
Edamame
Strawberries

FOOD ART INGREDIENTS

Hot dog
Ham
Pasta sticks
Nori

TOOLS NEEDED

Cling wrap
Round cutter
Craft punch
Tweezers
Knife
Scissors

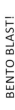

1. Remove crusts from the bread. Slice bread and hot dog in half. Place lettuce, chicken salad, and half of the hot dog on it as shown. Roll up the bread and wrap with cling wrap to hold. Set aside for a while.

2. Cut out two circles from a slice of ham using a round cutter or straw to form the bunny's paws. Using a knife or a pair of scissors, cut out the bunny's ears from the ham.

3. Use a knife to make a slit on top of the hot dog so that the ears can be inserted as shown. Attach the bunny's hands to the sandwich using pasta sticks.

4. Cut out the bunny's features from a sheet of nori using a craft punch.

Bunny Carrot

A little rabbit wiggles his nose and munches on his carrot in this sandwich bento. It will only take you a few minutes to craft and pack this rabbit for your child. The Japanese hamburg steak for this sandwich is packed separately, so your child can have the fun hands-on experience of assembling their own sandwich during lunchtime. A little cute bee made from a quail egg can also be added to brighten this bento.

BENTO MENU	FOOD ART INGREDIENTS	TOOLS NEEDED
Japanese hamburg steak (p. 217)	Bread	Scissors
Lettuce	Black olives	Knife
Spinach	Baby carrot	Leaf bento pick
Carrots	Honey/pasta sticks	Spoon
Sweet peas	Hard-boiled quail egg	Bowl
Carrots	Curry powder/turmeric	Tweezers
	Cheese	Craft punch
	Nori	Heart-shaped cutter

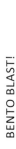

1. Using a knife or scissors, cut out the bunny's face, ears, and hands from bread.

2. Cut out the bunny's facial features from olives as shown.

3. Spread honey on the olive cutouts and place them on the sandwich, or secure using pasta sticks. Make diagonal cuts in baby carrots with a knife, and insert a leaf-shaped bento pick on top.

4. Mix curry powder or turmeric powder with hot water. Dip quail eggs in the dyed water until the desired yellow color is achieved.

5. Cut out strips of nori. Spread some honey on quail egg and wrap strips of nori around it.

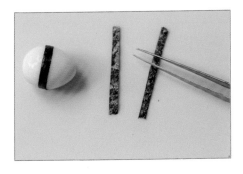

6. Using a craft punch, cut out the bee's eyes and mouth in a nori sheet. Use a heart-shaped cutter to cut out the cheese to make the bee's wings.

Seal Sandwich

With a little imagination, you can use a bear-shaped sandwich cutter to form adorable seals simply by turning them upside down! Complete this bento with an adorable little turtle made from kiwis and grapes. Pack this lunch with a gel pack so that everything is kept cool until lunchtime.

BENTO MENU

Carrots
Cucumbers
Cherry tomato
Yogurt

FOOD ART INGREDIENTS

Bread
Cheese
Ham
Nori
Kiwi

TOOLS NEEDED

CuteZCute Animal Friends
     sandwich cutter
Round cutter
Scissors
Nori punch
Tweezers

1. Use a bear-shaped sandwich cutter to make cutouts in two slices of bread, one slice of cheese, and one slice of ham. Assemble them one on top of the other as a sandwich.

2. Use a small round cutter to cut out two circles from the bread. Cut out a heart shape from the bread using a cutter or a pair of scissors.

3. Use a nori punch to cut out the seal's eyes, nose, and whiskers in a sheet of nori.

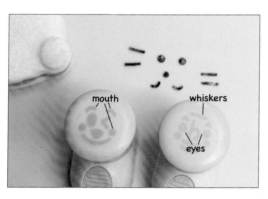

4. Use a round cutter on a slice of ham to cut out the seal's cheeks. Assemble all the parts into a seal as shown in the picture.

5. Use a slice of green kiwi as the turtle's body. Slice grapes in half to form the turtle's legs and head.

6. Arrange the turtle in a bento box that has been filled with yogurt. Using a pair of tweezers, add the turtle's eyes using the black seeds from the kiwi.

Mermaid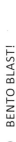

Does your little girl dream of transforming into a little mermaid? Learn the steps to craft this mermaid under the sea. In this bento, noodles are used for her soft, wavy hair. There are also instructions in this bento tutorial on how to make a ham flower, which serves as both filler and decoration for your bentos.

BENTO MENU
Nutella sandwich
Cajun spiced grilled wings
    (p. 208)
Carrots
Cucumbers
Salami
Cherry tomatoes
Lettuce

FOOD ART INGREDIENTS
Dark colored cheese
Light colored cheese
Ham
Nori
Noodles
Carrots
Pasta sticks

TOOLS NEEDED
Parchment paper
Pencil/marker
Scissors
Knife
Fish cutter
Tweezers
Paw craft punch

1. Trace out the mermaid figure (p. 246) on parchment paper and make a cutout in slices of dark-colored cheese, light-colored cheese, and ham as shown. Follow the instructions on how to cut out characters using a template (p. 17).

2. Use a paw craft punch to cut out ovals for the eyes from a sheet of nori. Use a pair of scissors to cut out 2 thin curved lines from nori to form her nose and mouth.

3. Arrange the mermaid on top of a Nutella sandwich. Add noodles tossed in a little soy sauce and sesame oil for her hair.

4. Using a fish-shaped cutter, cut out a fish from a slice of carrot.

5. Fold a salami in half. Using a knife, make cuts at regular intervals on the folded side as shown. You can also use ham instead of salami.

6. Roll up your salami as shown.

7. Secure using a pasta stick.

8. Using a knife, slice off the excess salami at the bottom so that the flower can stand on its base.

Sleeping Teddy Bear Sandwich

Sleep tight little bears, and sweet dreams! A trio of hot dog bears are tucked snugly under an egg omelette blankie. The bears are lying on a pillow cut out from carrots. The bed they are lying on is a sandwich filled with delicious chicken salad. Complete this lunch bento by packing another small box filled with veggies and fruits for a balanced, nutritious meal.

BENTO MENU

Chicken salad (p. 209)
Bread
Lettuce
Corn
Apple
Cucumbers
Carrots
Purple carrots

FOOD ART INGREDIENTS

Egg sheet
Hot dogs
Nori
Cheese
Carrots
Pasta sticks

TOOLS NEEDED

Knife
Round cutter
Paw craft punch
Tweezers
Star cutter

1. Use a rectangular bento box to make an imprint on the bread, before cutting it using a knife. Spread chicken salad between slices of bread to form a sandwich. Line edges with lettuce.

2. Slice a mini hot dog in half, using one half for the bear's body. Use a small round cutter to cut circles from the other half of the sausage. These will form the bear's ears and hands.

3. Use the round cutter to cut a circle from a slice of cheese for the bear's snout.

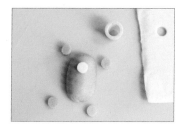

4. Cut out ovals from a sheet of nori using a craft punch to form the bear's eyes and nose.

5. Slice an egg sheet to fit in the bento box. Fold down the top of the egg sheet to resemble the fold of the blanket.

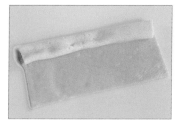

6. Slice carrots into rectangles using a knife, to be used as pillows for the bears.

7. Arrange carrot pillows, followed by hot dog bears, using pasta sticks to secure them to their sandwich bed. Cover them with the egg sheet blanket. Secure the bear's hands onto the egg sheet using pasta sticks.

8. Cut out stars from purple carrots using a star-shaped cutter.

Cat and Yarn Pita

Pita is a delicious Mediterranean flatbread that adds variety to your usual lunch menu. It also allows you to experiment with different fillings. In this fusion recipe, fill your pita pockets with lettuce and chicken teriyaki. Use hard-boiled quail eggs to make cute little kitties who play with yarn on the pita. You can dye the eggs in lovely pink and blue shades using natural ingredients.

BENTO MENU	FOOD ART INGREDIENTS	TOOLS NEEDED
Pita pocket	Hard-boiled quail eggs	Cling wrap
Chicken teriyaki (p. 205)	Pasta sticks	Craft punch
Lettuce	Beetroot	Tweezers
Carrots	Red cabbage	Scissors
Cherry tomato	Nori	Knife
Noodles	Mayonnaise	

1. Cut out a center piece of the bread bun as shown above. Do not cut all the way—leave the base intact. Fill your bun with whatever fillings you prefer. I filled mine with tuna salad.

2. Boil the hot dog and slice it into eight small pieces, four for the wheels and two for the bear car's ears. If you find the hot dogs too big for your bear's ears, you can make a smaller cutout in the hot dog slice using a small round cutter.

3. Attach the car's wheels and the bear car's ears with pasta sticks. Cut out ovals for the bear car's eyes and a circle for its nose from a slice of cheese.

4. Using a round cutter or a straw, cut out the bear car's cheeks from a slice of ham. Use a nori punch to cut out the bear car's eyes and nose from a sheet of nori.

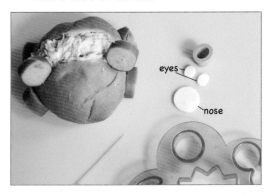

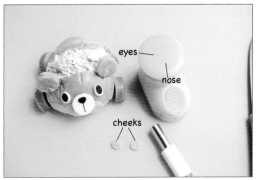

5. To make the steering wheel, cut the slice of cheese with a round cutter. Then, cut the circle of cheese in half to make a semicircle. Use a toothpick to carve out the ring shape of the wheel.

6. Lay the cheese on a sheet of nori and cut the nori following the outline of the cheese. Use a bear-shaped cutter to cut out the bear's head from the cheese and use a paw craft punch to cut out ovals from the nori for his eyes and nose.

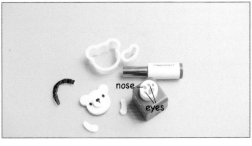

Tiger Bread Buns

Rawr! These tigers aren't fierce at all. Friendly little tigers are made using bread buns and packed alongside hearty chicken stew, which is kept warm in a thermal container until lunchtime. Food like stews are great for packing in thermal containers, as they will continue to slow-cook in the containers.

BENTO MENU

White wine chicken stew
(p. 203)
Lettuce
Kiwi
Strawberries
Red currants

FOOD ART INGREDIENTS

Bread buns
Nori
Cheese
Mayonnaise

TOOLS NEEDED

Knife
Round cutter/piping tip
Oval cutter
Scissors
Tweezers

1. Slice off the bottom of the bread bun.

2. Use this portion to cut out the tiger's ears using a round cutter. If you do not have a round cutter, you can use the back of a piping tip.

3. Make a slit in the bread bun using a knife, then slot in the ears.

4. Using a pair of scissors, cut out the tiger's features from a sheet of nori as shown.

5. Dab on some mayonnaise as "glue" and use a pair of tweezers to place the nori on the bread bun.

6. Use an oval cutter to cut out the tiger's cheeks from a slice of cheese and place on the bread buns.

Hot Dog Bread Bun

In this twist on the classic hot dog bun, these buns hold a little adorable dog that will bring a smile to your child's face as he or she opens their bento box. Complete this meal with a healthy side of veggies and fruits.

BENTO MENU

Bread rolls
Lettuce
Carrots
Cucumbers
Cherry tomato
Kiwis
Grapes
Strawberries

FOOD ART INGREDIENTS

Hot dog
Nori
Pasta sticks
Mayonnaise

TOOLS NEEDED

Knife
Scissors
Tweezers
Paw craft punch
Nori punch

1. Slice the hot dog in half along its length. Take one half, and slice off one third of it for the dog's head.

2. Slice away the skin of the hot dog third using a knife.

3. Cut out ears and tail from the skin of the hot dog using a pair of scissors.

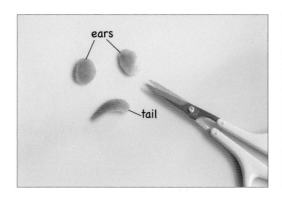

4. Fill your buns with lettuce and a hot dog. You can also stuff leftover hot dog cutouts in the bun so as not to waste food.

5. Use pasta sticks to attach the dog's head, ears, and tail onto the hot dog. Use a nori punch to cut out the dog's eyes and nose from a sheet of nori. Spread some mayonnaise as "glue" before placing the nori cutouts on the hot dog.

Owl Bread Buns

A pair of sleepy owls, who should be sleeping during the day, are rudely awakened as your child opens his packed lunch! Are you as exhausted as they are in the morning too? Try this bento box idea that requires no cooking, making it easier for you to put them together on a sleepy morning.

BENTO MENU	FOOD ART INGREDIENTS	TOOLS NEEDED
Ham buns	Bread buns	Round cutters
Cucumbers	Dark colored cheese	Petal cutter
Carrots	Light colored cheese	Tweezers
Kiwis	Nori	Scissors
Strawberries	Mayonnaise	Nori punch

1. Slice buns in half, spread with cream cheese, and layer with shredded ham and lettuce.

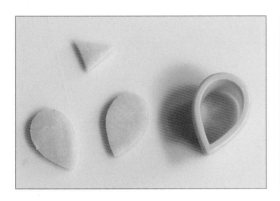

2. Use two differently sized round cutters to make cutouts in light colored cheese as shown.

3. Use a petal cutter to make cutouts in a slice of dark colored cheese. Use a knife to cut out a small triangle as well.

4. Use a nori punch to cut out feather details in a sheet of nori. Use a pair of scissors to cut out two circles from the nori for the eyes. Assemble the different parts on the bun using pasta sticks and mayonnaise, if needed.

5. Use a round cutter to make circular cutouts in the dark colored cheese. Slice the cheese circle in half and place over the owl's eyes as hooded lids.

Dog Burger 🍞

Kids love burgers and puppies, so make a healthy hamburger filled with homemade beef patties and spinach that is shaped like a dog. To make beef patties, adapt my meatball pasta recipe by shaping the meatballs into patties instead. This bento is packed with a warming pumpkin soup that features a hint of curry perfect for rainy days or cool weather. Pack the soup in a thermal container to keep it warm for your child until lunchtime.

BENTO MENU	FOOD ART INGREDIENTS	TOOLS NEEDED
Beef patties (p. 234, steps 1–3, 5)	Dark colored cheese	Knife
Spinach	Light colored cheese	Round cutters
Curry pumpkin soup (p. 237)	Black olives	Scissors
	Pasta sticks	Tweezers
		Toothpicks

1. Using a knife, slice bread buns in half.

2. Place the bottom bun in the bento box and place beef patties and spinach on it.

3. Using a round cutter, cut out a circle from a slice of light colored cheese. Using a knife, toothpick, or a pair of scissors, cut out oval-shaped ears from dark colored cheese.

ears

4. Using a pair of scissors, cut out eyes, nose, and mouth from olives. Attach them onto the burger using pasta sticks.

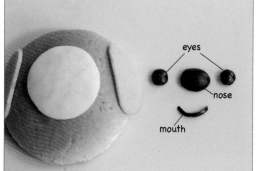

eyes

nose

mouth

Astronaut

Three, two, one...blast off! Do you have a little astronaut wannabe at home? This astronaut bento will be perfect for him or her. Here, you will learn the steps to craft the astronaut, rocket, and the USA flag as well to complete this space-themed bento.

BENTO MENU

Ham and cream cheese
    sandwich
Corn
Carrots
Cucumbers
Lettuce

FOOD ART INGREDIENTS

Bread buns
Ham
Cheese
Nori
Red bell peppers
Apples
Blueberries
Pasta sticks
Honey

TOOLS NEEDED

Knife
Scissors
Toothpick
Paw craft punch
Nori punch
Tweezers
Round cutter/straw

1. Slice bread bun in half.

2. Using a knife, cut out a rectangle in the middle of one half of the bread bun. Place a slice of ham on the other half, trimming ham to fit.

3. Using a toothpick, cut out the astronaut's hair from a slice of cheese, as shown in the picture.

4. Assemble the bread, ham, and cheese as shown to make the astronaut's head. Spread cream cheese on the bread that forms the helmet.

5. Cut out two strips of bell peppers and place them on the helmet.

6. Use a paw craft punch to cut out the astronaut's eyes from a sheet of nori. Use a nori punch to cut out his nose and mouth from the nori.

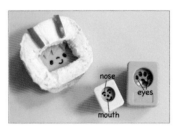

7. Cut out the astronaut's body, hands, and part of the helmet from a slice of bread, as shown in the picture.

8. Spread cream cheese on the body and hands. Cut out rectangle shapes from a slice of cheese and a red bell pepper and place on the body.

9. Assemble all parts in the bento box.

10. Cut out a rectangular slice of apple. Using a knife, make parallel cuts on the apple as shown.

11. Use the knife to remove alternating strips of apple skin. Soak the apple in salted water or spray with lemon juice to prevent it from browning.

12. Assemble the apple in the bento box and add blueberries in the top left hand corner. This will form the American flag. You can use honey as "glue" to prevent the blueberries from shifting.

13. Cut out a rectangular piece of cheese and triangular red bell peppers to form the rocket as shown. Secure the different parts together using pasta sticks.

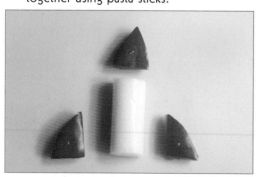

14. Cut out circles from cheese and place on the rocket.

Bento and Food Art Tutorials

SALAD AND NOODLE BENTOS

Sleeping Bunny Salad 🍚

Eggs can be molded and shaped while they are still hot, so why not shape them into a dainty pair of bunnies? Arrange a pair of blissful bunnies sleeping on top of a bed of salad that will entice your child to eat his or her greens.

BENTO MENU

Salad with dressing
Salmon mayonnaise
  (p. 221)
Grilled bell peppers
Berries

FOOD ART INGREDIENTS

Quail eggs
Nori
Pink cake decorating gel
Pasta sticks
Mayonnaise

TOOLS NEEDED

Knife
Cling wrap
Nori punch
Tweezers
Scissors

1. Soon after hard boiling, wrap a hard-boiled quail egg in cling wrap. Secure it by twisting the ends and molding it into a round shape while it is still hot. Dip in ice cold water once you are happy with the shape of the egg. Remove once it has fully cooled down. Slice the quail egg in half and use it for the bunny's head.

2. Use the other half of the hard-boiled quail egg for the bunny's body.

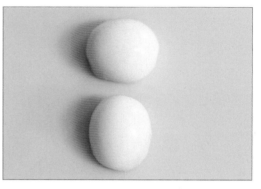

3. Using another quail egg, cut out the bunny's ears and legs as shown.

4. Cut out the bunny's eyes and nose from a sheet of nori using a nori punch or a pair of scissors.

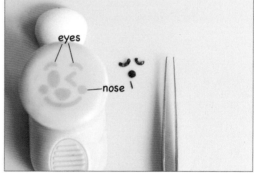

eyes

nose

5. Dab on some mayonnaise as "glue" before attaching the nori cutouts on the bunny. Dab on some pink cake decorating gel for the bunny's cheeks.

Cow Salad

Two cows graze on a bed of salad. These cows are made from hard-boiled eggs. The side dish for this bento is honey chicken, which is cut into small pieces so that your child can toss it together with the salad during mealtime. You will also learn to cut checkered apples, which look great as a delicious and nutritional filler in any bento box.

BENTO MENU

Salad with dressing
Honey chicken (p. 214)
Apple

FOOD ART INGREDIENTS

Hard-boiled egg
Nori
Dark colored cheese
Light colored cheese
Mayonnaise

TOOLS NEEDED

Knife
Tweezers
Scissors
Round cutters

1. Use a round cutter to make cutouts in dark colored cheese and light colored cheese. Use the lighter cheese circle as the base. Use the round cutter and make an overlapping cut in the darker cheese circle to create a pointed oval as shown.

2. Use a small round cutter or straw to cut a circle in the dark colored cheese and slice it in half to form the cow's ears.

3. Slice the hard-boiled egg in half. Place the cheese cutouts on one half. Use a nori punch to cut out the eyes and nostrils from nori. Dab on mayonnaise as "glue" and use tweezers to place cutouts on the egg.

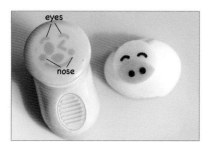

4. Use a pair of scissors to cut out cow patches from the nori and place on the egg using the tweezers.

5. Carve vertical and horizontal lines into the apple skin until you form a grid pattern.

6. Use the tip of your knife to remove alternating squares of the skin to turn the grid into a checkered pattern.

7. Soak the apple in salted water or spray with lemon juice to prevent it from browning.

Quail Egg Mice 🍱

Two little mice nibble a slice of real cheese in this bento. To top things off, the mice are served on top of creamy carbonara pasta, a delicious and savory staple. Cut out carrots in a waffle shape so that they are more fun for the children to eat. This bento is full of healthy vegetable side dishes such as zucchini, corn, carrots, and cherry tomatoes.

BENTO MENU

Chicken carbonara
(p. 233)
Zucchini and tomato
baked with cheese
(p. 227)
Corn
Carrots
Cherry tomato

FOOD ART INGREDIENTS

Hard-boiled quail eggs
Cheddar cheese
Nori
Hot dog
Pasta sticks
Peas

TOOLS NEEDED

Knife
Scissors
Craft punch
Round cutters
Tweezers

1. Prepare a hard-boiled quail egg and a cooked hot dog. Cut two slices of the hot dog to be used as ears.

2. Using a knife, make a slit in the quail egg to slot in the hot dog ears. Use pasta sticks to attach a pea to the quail egg for the mouse's nose.

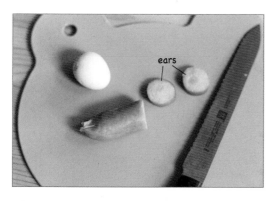

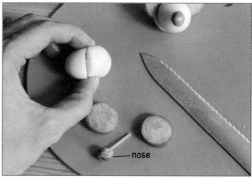

3. Using a craft punch or a pair of scissors, cut out the mouse's eyes from a sheet of nori. Use pasta sticks for the mouse's whiskers. Fry the pasta sticks if you are going to eat them immediately after preparation.

4. Using a knife, cut out a triangular slice of cheese. Use a round cutter or straw to poke holes in the cheese.

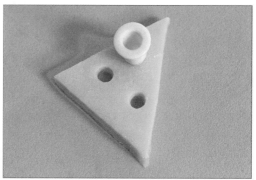

Pesto Pasta Frog

Pack this healthy pesto pasta bento for your kid's lunch, and turn it into a cute frog in just a few simple steps. Pesto can be made ahead of time and stored in the refrigerator for around a week. To store it longer, you can freeze pesto in individual portions and use when needed. This bento also comes with cheesy side dishes that will have your child looking forward to lunch!

BENTO MENU	FOOD ART INGREDIENTS	TOOLS NEEDED
Pesto pasta (p. 237)	Cherry tomato	Round cutters
Cheese baked shrimp (p. 223)	Cheese	Toothpicks
	Nori	Scissors
Zucchini and tomato baked with cheese (p. 227)		Tweezers

1. Pack one section of the bento box with pesto pasta.

2. Using a round cutter, cut out circles from a slice of cheese.

3. Cut out the frog's eyes and mouth from a sheet of nori using a pair of scissors.

4. Place the mouth cutout on a slice of cheese. Use a toothpick to cut out the outline of the mouth in the cheese.

eyes

mouth

5. Assemble the parts on the pasta. Add sliced halves of a cherry tomato for the cheeks.

Meatball Pasta Bear

Kids love meatballs, especially with spaghetti tossed in a tomato-based sauce. Use pasta to form the bear's face and shape two meatballs as the bear's ears before cooking them. Your little one will be thrilled when he or she is greeted by this delicious pasta bear during lunch at school.

BENTO MENU

Meatball pasta (p. 234)
Cherry tomato
Hard-boiled egg
Blanched broccoli

FOOD ART INGREDIENTS

Meatball
Cheese
Nori

TOOLS NEEDED

Scissors
Tweezers
Oval cutter
Round cutters

1. When shaping meatballs for panfrying, shape two smaller ones to be used as the bear's ears. Pack a section of the bento box with pasta.

2. Cut out two ovals for the eyes and a circle for the snout from a slice of cheese using cutters.

3. Using a pair of scissors, cut out bear's features from a sheet of nori.

4. Use a small round cutter or a straw to cut out two circles from cheese for the bear's eyes.

5. Assemble the different cutouts and secure with pasta sticks if needed.

Shrimp Snail Pad Thai

Pad thai is a stir-fried shrimp noodle dish from Thailand, seasoned using fish sauce and chili powder, and tossed with peanuts. Omit chili for a more kid-friendly version if your children cannot take spicy food. Make use of the shrimps used in pad thai to make a pair of friendly snails.

BENTO MENU	FOOD ART INGREDIENTS	TOOLS NEEDED
Pad thai (p. 236)	Shrimp	Toothpick
Kiwis	Cheese	Tweezers
Strawberries	Nori	Nori punch
	Fried pasta sticks	
	Pink food decorating gel	
	Peas	

1. Cut a teardrop shape from a slice of cheese using a toothpick.

2. Using a nori punch, cut out eyes and mouth from a sheet of nori.

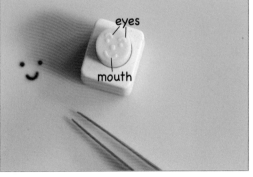

eyes

mouth

3. Assemble the cheese and nori cutouts as shown, adding a pea in the middle of the shrimp and two fried pasta sticks on the head. Dab pink food decorating gel on the cheese for pink cheeks. Place in your bento on the pad thai.

Bento and Food Art Tutorials

SPECIAL OCCASIONS

Sushi Birthday Cake

Celebrate your child's birthday with a savory rice birthday cake! This cake is layered with sushi rice and smoked salmon, then decorated using mashed potatoes to form a bunny in a field of flowers. Mashed potatoes are not just great for molding characters; they can also be used in piping bags to make various designs on your bento, just like a cake decoration.

BENTO MENU
Smoked salmon

FOOD ART INGREDIENTS
Rice
Mashed potatoes
  (p. 177, steps 1 and 2)
Pink food gel coloring/
  beetroot

TOOLS NEEDED
"Happy Birthday"
  cupcake topper
Small round cake tin
Toothpick
Cling wrap
Nori punch
Paw craft punch
Tweezers
Wax paper
Ribbon
Piping bag with star tip

1. You need a small round cake tin or any small round container. Line with cling wrap and fill with a layer of rice. Use cling wrap to gently press the rice down to compact.

2. Layer with smoked salmon and top with another layer of rice. Use cling wrap to gently press the rice down to compact. You can add another layer of smoked salmon and rice, if preferred.

3. Lift out the cling wrap slowly to remove the rice cake, place on a plate, and remove the cling wrap carefully. Wrap wax paper around the sides and secure by tying a ribbon around it.

4. Prepare mashed potatoes. Scoop out 1 tbsp of mashed potatoes and set aside. Color the rest with pink food gel coloring using a toothpick.

5. You can also color the mashed potato naturally using mashed beetroot. Add beetroot a little at a time until you get your desired shade. Mashed potatoes can be prepared a day in advance and stored in the fridge.

6. Using your colored mashed potato, shape the bunny's body parts and place on cling wrap.

7. Attach on the ears by pressing gently. Using the mashed potato set aside in step 4, mold out a round shape for the bunny's nose and attach it to the bunny's head by pressing gently.

8. Using a nori punch and a craft punch, cut out the eyes and nose from a sheet of nori.

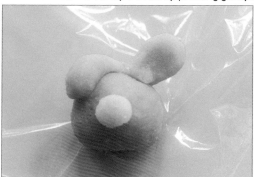

9. Arrange the bunny onto the rice cake as shown. For now, leave out the hands.

10. Place a "Happy Birthday" cupcake topper onto the cake and place the bunny's hands over it.

11. Roll up smoked salmon to make roses.

12. Place the salmon roses onto the rice cake. Fill mashed potatoes into a piping bag attached with a star-shaped tip. Pipe out flowers onto the rice cake.

Mother's Day Hen
and Chicks

Make this mother hen and baby chicks bento to celebrate Mother's Day. Prepare this bento together with your kids for a great bonding activity; plus they will be packing a bento for you this time around! One of the side dishes here is teriyaki chicken. Teriyaki is a cooking technique used in Japanese cuisine where food is broiled or grilled with a glaze of soy sauce, mirin, and sugar. The result is a sweet and savory sauce that goes very well with most food.

BENTO MENU

Chicken teriyaki (p. 205)
Pea shoots and mushroom
    stir-fry (p. 231)

FOOD ART INGREDIENTS

Rice
Hard-boiled egg
Corn
Ham
Nori
Pasta sticks

TOOLS NEEDED

Wax paper
Cling wrap
Heart-shaped bento
    picks
Hat bento picks
Scissors
Knife
Tweezers
Nori punch
Oval cutter

1. Mix rice with mashed hard-boiled egg yolk to color it a natural yellow.

2. Using cling wrap, shape rice into two oval rice balls.

3. Use an oval cutter to cut out the chick's cheeks from a slice of ham. Use a nori punch to cut out the chick's eyes and feet from a sheet of nori.

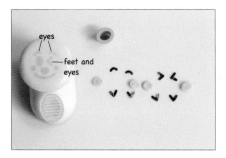

4. Assemble the parts with tweezers. Use pasta sticks to attach the ham cutouts. Use a heart-shaped bento pick for the chick's beak. Add a hat bento pick.

5. Shape an oval rice ball using white rice and cling wrap. Using a knife or a pair of scissors, cut out the shapes as shown in the picture from egg white. Cut out the shape of an apron from a slice of ham.

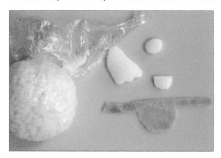

6. Using pasta sticks, attach kernels of cooked corn to the rice ball for the hen's beak. Using a nori punch, cut out circles from a sheet of nori for the hen's eyes.

7. Attach on the various parts with the help of pasta sticks.

8. Cut out a piece of wax paper and wrap it around the hen's head as her scarf.

Father's Day

Racking your brains on how to make something special for Father's Day? Why not let your kids express their appreciation for Dad by getting them to make a bento just for him? Help the little ones craft out a shirt sandwich for their dearest Daddy—if he works in an office, that is!

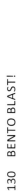
BENTO MENU

Chicken salad (p. 209)

Lettuce

Grated cheese

Carrots

Celery

Ranch dressing

Yogurt

Strawberries

FOOD ART INGREDIENTS

Bread

Dark colored cheese

Light colored cheese

Pasta sticks

TOOLS NEEDED

Knife

Rolling pin

1. Place the sandwich fillings of chicken salad, lettuce, and grated cheese on a slice of bread. Cut the top slice in half. Replace both halves on top of the sandwich.

2. Remove the crust from another slice of bread. Roll it flat using a rolling pin.

3. Cut bread into half strips using a knife.

4. Arrange the strips as a collar on the sandwich, and secure using pasta sticks if needed.

5. Make a tie cutout in a dark colored cheese as shown. Cut strips from a light colored cheese to form the tie's stripes.

6. Arrange the tie on the sandwich. Fill the first remaining box with carrots, celery, and ranch dressing; and the second with yogurt and strawberries.

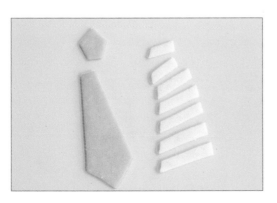

Christmas Santa

Ho ho ho! A Santa bento is perfect for the Christmas holiday season. This bento even includes a cute little snowman made out of quail eggs. A Hamburg steak, a Japanese interpretation of a Western hamburger patty, is packed as a side dish. It is made from a blend of beef and pork that has been glazed in a sweet and savory sauce and is commonly served with rice.

BENTO MENU

Japanese hamburg steak
  (p. 217)
Sesame broccoli (p. 227)
Squash stir-fry (p. 228)

FOOD ART INGREDIENTS

Rice
Hard-boiled quail eggs
Ham
Nori
Red bell peppers
Cauliflower
Cheese
Ketchup
Pasta sticks

TOOLS NEEDED

Cling wrap
Tweezers
Knife
Round cutter/straw
Nori punch
Craft punch
Hat bento pick

1. Mix rice with ketchup to color pink. Use cling wrap to shape rice into a rice ball.

2. Cut out Santa's hat as shown in the picture using a slice of cheese and a red bell pepper. Use a small round cutter or straw to cut out the circle for the top of the hat.

3. Arrange Santa in the bento box, using blanched cauliflower as his beard.

4. Make a round cutout in a red bell pepper using a round cutter. Cut out Santa's eyes from a sheet of nori using a nori punch.

5. Wrap cling wrap round a hard-boiled quail egg while it's still warm to shape it round. Dip it in ice water to cool it down after it's been shaped.

6. Use a craft punch to cut a sheet of nori for the snowman's features.

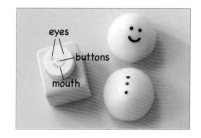

7. Cut out a strip of ham for the snowman's scarf. Attach the quail eggs together using a pasta stick.

8. Wrap ham around the snowman and secure with a pasta stick. Stick a hat bento pick onto his head to complete his look.

Wintery Snowman

A jolly snowman is another idea for the festive holiday season. Create this sweet cream cheese snowman sandwich out of delicious fruits and chocolate. Additionally, what is Christmas without presents from your loved ones? Learn to make edible presents using cheese and ham, for a nutritional side dish.

BENTO MENU

Cajun spiced grilled wings
   (p. 208)
Lettuce
Christmas pasta
Red currants

FOOD ART INGREDIENTS

Bread buns
Cream cheese
Strawberries
Blueberries
Chocolate chips
Chocolate sprinkles
Apple
Colby Jack cheese
Ham

TOOLS NEEDED

Knife
Tweezers
Heart-shaped bento pick

1. Slice bread buns in half. Spread cream cheese on the bread buns.

2. Cut a slice of strawberry into a triangle for the snowman's nose. Using tweezers, place chocolate chips for the snowman's eyes and chocolate sprinkles for his mouth.

strawberry

chocolate chip

chocolate sprinkle

3. Add blueberries for the snowman's buttons and slice another triangle of strawberry for his hat.

strawberry

blueberry

4. To make the snowman's scarf, slice an apple as shown into three strips. Make "V"-shaped cuts at the ends of two of the strips.

5. Make shallow slanted cuts in the apple's skin. Use a knife to remove alternating skins on the apple. Soak apples in salted water or spray with lemon juice to prevent browning.

6. Assemble the snowman in the bento box.

7. Cut out a cube of cheese and two long strips of ham.

8. Wrap the ham strips around the cheese to resemble a present and secure by sticking a heart bento pick through the top.

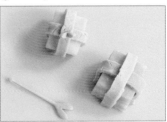

Spooky Halloween

Prepare a not-so-frightful Halloween bento box for your kids during this spooky season! Pack a friendly ghost for your child to bring to school. The jack-o'-lantern is made from rice that has been mixed with steamed mashed pumpkin, but it can also be made purely from mashed pumpkin. The side dish of chicken veggie rolls in this bento is not only beautiful, but also tastes delicious.

BENTO MENU	FOOD ART INGREDIENTS	TOOLS NEEDED
Chicken veggie roll (p. 204)	Rice	Cling wrap
Green bean omelette (p. 224)	Steamed pumpkin	Tweezers
Grilled tomatoes	Nori	Spoon
Lettuce	Cheese	Leaf bento pick
	Carrot	Scissors
	Ketchup	Nori punch
		Toothpick
		Chopstick

1. Mix mashed steamed pumpkin with rice to dye it orange.

2. Using cling wrap, shape rice into a rice ball. Use a spoon to make parallel indentations on the rice.

3. Cut out the jack-o'-lantern's facial features from nori using scissors. Use tweezers to place the nori cutouts on the rice.

4. Stick a leaf bento pick in the pumpkin rice ball and dab on some ketchup for its cheeks.

5. Using cling wrap, shape more rice into an oval rice ball. Place rice ball in a food cup.

6. Use a nori punch to cut out eyes, mouth, and hands for the ghost from a sheet of nori.

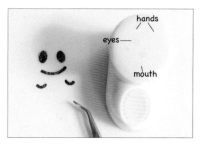

7. Cut out a hat shape from a sheet of nori and a strip of cheese to make a hat. Place them on a slice of cheese and cut along the hat's outline using a toothpick.

8. Cut out a small oval from a slice of carrot using a cutter for the ghost's tongue. Assemble the parts on the rice ball as shown. Dab on ketchup using a chopstick to form the ghost's cheeks.

Halloween Monster and Mummy Sandwich 🧁

Can't get hold of green bread? No worries; just use a guacamole spread on your bread to turn it green and transform your sandwich into a monster that's perfect for Halloween. Add a mummy sandwich to complete this spooky bento box. This bento is packed with a side dish of homemade chicken nuggets, which are so yummy that your kids will soon be asking for more.

BENTO MENU

Guacamole sandwich
Nutella sandwich
Chicken nuggets (p. 203)
Grapes
Carrots
Lettuce

FOOD ART INGREDIENTS

Cheese
Blueberries
Bread
Pasta sticks
Nutella or melted
    chocolate

TOOLS NEEDED

Knife
Tweezers
Scissors
Round cutters
Rolling pin

1. Using a knife or a pair of scissors, cut out the monster's jagged hair in a zigzag fashion from bread crust, or the heels of the bread in a loaf.

2. Spread guacamole on a slice of bread and place the bread crust cutout on top.

3. Cut circles from cheese using a round cutter. Add two blueberries and secure onto the sandwich using pasta sticks.

4. Fill a piping bag with Nutella or melted chocolate and use it to draw on the monster's mouth and scar.

5. Make a round cutout in another slice of bread using a round cutter.

6. Spread on Nutella. Cut out circles from cheese using a round cutter.

7. Roll another slice of bread flat using a rolling pin.

8. Place cheese circles on the sandwich followed by two blueberries for the eyes. Secure using pasta sticks. Cut strips from the rolled out bread and place on the sandwich to make the mummy's burial cloth. Trim off excess.

Easter Chicks
in Bunny Suits

Celebrate Eater with this adorable chick bento. Some of these chicks even don a bunny suit for the occasion! Learn to craft chicks and their bunny suits using quail eggs, and their nest using rice and shaved bonito flakes, a dried, smoked fish condiment that is often sprinkled on tofu for extra flavor.

BENTO MENU

Cajun spiced grilled wings
  (p. 208)
Strawberries
Lettuce

FOOD ART INGREDIENTS

Rice
Shaved bonito flakes
Hard-boiled quail eggs
Carrot
Nori
Pink cake decorating gel
Pasta sticks
Mayonnaise

TOOLS NEEDED

Cling wrap
Knife
Tweezers
Round cutter
Oval cutter
Paw craft punch
"V"-shaped knife or small
  knife

1. To make chicks dressed in bunny suits, use an oval cutter to carefully make a shallow cut into the egg white portion of a hard-boiled quail egg.

2. Slowly peel off the egg white using a knife.

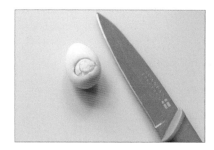

3. Scoop out a bit of the egg yolk and mix with mayonnaise. Use a knife to spread the egg yolk back into the hole we had cut out in the previous step.

4. Slice off a bit of egg white from another hard-boiled quail egg. Use an oval cutter to cut out the bunny's ears.

5. Attach the ears using pasta sticks.

6. Use a craft punch to cut out ovals in a sheet of nori for the eyes. Use a pair of scissors to cut out a small straight line for the bunny's mouth.

7. Cut out the chick's beak from a slice of carrot using an oval cutter. Dab on pink cake decorating gel to form the cheeks for both the bunny and the chick.

8. To make chicks, dye peeled hard-boiled quail eggs yellow by adding curry powder to water (p. 16).

9. Use a craft punch to cut out ovals from a sheet of nori for the eyes. Use an oval cutter to cut out ovals from a slice of carrot for the beak.

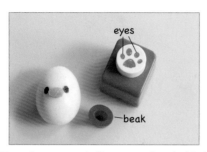

11. To make an egg shell on top of a chick's head, use a "V"-shaped knife or a small knife to make zigzagged cuts along the entire length of a hard-boiled egg.

13. To make the nest, form a rice ball using cling wrap. Slowly press down in the middle to shape the nest.

15. If you cannot get hold of bonito flakes, you can arrange pasta in a round container to form the nest instead.

10. To make the chick's feet, first cut a long straight line from nori using scissors. Snip the nori strip into smaller bits. Use tweezers to arrange the nori on the quail egg as shown. Use mayonnaise as "glue" to stick.

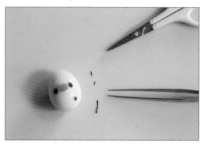

12. Place "egg shell" on the yellow quail egg and complete the chick in the same way as shown in previous steps, with nori cutouts for eyes and feet, carrot cutouts for beak, and cake decorating gel for the cheeks.

14. Coat the rice in bonito flakes to complete the nest.

Valentine's Day Rose Wrap

A bouquet of roses is always a welcome gift on Valentine's Day. To celebrate, how about a rose bouquet ham sandwich and a love letter sandwich that can be eaten? Complete this love-themed bento with heart-shaped tomatoes.

BENTO MENU

Ham
Lettuce
Hard-boiled egg
Cucumbers
Mayonnaise

FOOD ART INGREDIENTS

Bread—preferably one
 white and one brown
Thinly sliced ham
Lettuce
Strawberry
Cherry tomatoes
Pasta sticks

TOOLS NEEDED

Wax paper
String
Rolling pin
Heart cutter
Knife

1. To make the rose bouquet sandwich, slice off bread crust and roll a slice of white bread flat using a rolling pin.

2. Fold a round piece of thinly sliced ham in half.

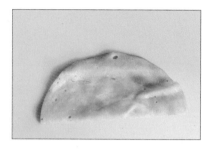

3. Roll up the ham and you will see a rose forming.

4. Secure the ham together using pasta sticks.

5. Arrange the lettuce and ham roses on the bread.

6. Fold two sides of the bread together to form a cone and secure with pasta sticks.

7. Wrap the bread with a piece of wax paper and tie with a string to secure.

8. To make the love letter, use a knife to slice a piece of brown bread into a rectangle and a triangle.

9. Using a heart-shaped cutter, make a cutout in a strawberry.

10. Assemble the bread and strawberry heart together and secure using pasta sticks.

11. Slice a cherry tomato diagonally in half.

12. Turn one side of the tomato upside down and secure them together using pasta sticks.

13. A heart-shaped tomato is formed.

Back to School

An owl teacher welcomes your little one back to school, putting a cheerful smile on his or her face. This ham owl sits on the cover of a book, reminding your child of the importance of doing homework! Follow these step-by-step photos to craft books, with covers made from a wrap and pages made from ham and cheese.

BENTO MENU

Ham and cheese wrap
Tamagoyaki (p. 225)
Carrots
Grapes
Strawberries
Lettuce

FOOD ART INGREDIENTS

Tortilla wrap
Dark colored ham
Light colored ham
Cooked pasta
Nori
Dark colored cheese
Light colored cheese
Carrot
Mayonnaise

TOOLS NEEDED

Knife
Round cutter/straw
Scissors
Tweezers
Parchment paper
Toothpick
Alphabet cutters
Blackboard cupcake
    topper
"You're #1" cupcake
    topper

1. Using a knife, slice a wrap into two rectangles.

2. Cut out rectangles in slices of light colored ham, dark colored ham, and cheese.

3. Stack the two pieces of the wrap one on top of the other. I am creating two books here. Using a round cutter or a straw, poke holes along the left side of the wrap.

4. Tie a knot at the end of a strand of cooked pasta. Thread pasta through the holes to secure the pieces of wraps together.

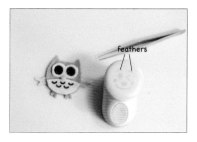

5. Insert ham and cheese into the wraps and assemble them in the bento box.

6. Cut out an owl from a slice of ham and cheese using the template (p. 246). Using a nori punch, cut out feathers in nori for the owl's breast. Use scissors to cut out circles in the nori for the eyes.

7. Use a toothpick to dab mayonnaise in the owl's eyes to form highlights.

8. Cut out alphabets from carrots using alphabet cutters.

Bento and Food Art Tutorials

SEASONAL BENTOS

Spring Sunflower Bee

Spring is when the flowers start to bloom. Capture this scene in your bento, with blooming sunflowers and a buzzing bee busy collecting nectar. In this bento, meat patty hamburg steaks are shaped into ovals and covered with a slice of cheese when cooking for melted cheesy goodness. Details are then added to craft it into a buzzing bee.

BENTO MENU
Rice
Japanese hamburg steak
    (p. 217)
Broccoli
Strawberries
Carrots

FOOD ART INGREDIENTS
Ham sausage
Cheese
Nori
Cucumber
Egg sheet
Ketchup
Pasta sticks

TOOLS NEEDED
Knife
Cupcake case
Scissors
Tweezers
Paw craft punch
Chopstick

1. Slice off a piece of ham and make crisscross cuts in its surface.

2. Heat pan with a little oil and panfry ham. Flip it and cook until both sides are lightly browned and the crisscross design is obvious.

3. Fill a cupcake case or food cup with rice.

4. Make egg sheets (p. 14). Fold them in half and make small parallel cuts around ¼-inch (½ cm) intervals apart in the egg sheet as shown in the picture, using a knife or scissors

5. Roll the egg sheet around the ham and secure with pasta sticks. The cuts in the egg sheet should fan out like a flower. Arrange on top of the rice.

6. Place sunflowers in bento box.

7. Shape meat patties into oval shapes and panfry them. Each patty will make one bee, so prepare according to the number of bees you want in your bento.

8. When both sides of the patties are browned, place cheese onto each patty while it's still cooking in the pan so that the cheese will melt and mold onto the meat patty.

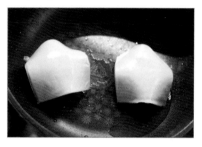

9. Using a pair of scissors, cut out strips from a sheet of nori.

10. Place nori onto the cheese meatball using a pair of tweezers.

11. Using a nori punch, cut out the bee's eyes and mouth from a sheet of nori.

12. Make bee's wings by slicing a cucumber and making a "V" cut in the edge.

13. Place cucumber onto the bee and attach on using pasta sticks. Use a chopstick to dab on ketchup for the bee's cheeks.

Summer Girl

When the weather is blazing hot and the sun is high in the sky, you know that it is summer. Another sure sign that summer is in full swing is when watermelons start popping up in your grocery store. This summer bento features a girl munching on a slice of watermelon. Her watermelon is actually made from cucumbers and carrots.

BENTO MENU

Black pepper chicken
  (p. 213)
Asparagus and corn
  stir-fry (p. 231)
Lettuce
Grapes
Strawberries

FOOD ART INGREDIENTS

Rice
Ketchup
Red cake decorating gel
Nori
Egg sheet (p. 14)
Cucumber
Carrot
Black sesame seeds
Pasta sticks
Mayonnaise

TOOLS NEEDED

Cling wrap
Knife
Scissors
Nori punch
Tweezers
Round cutter
Chopstick

1. Mix ketchup with rice to color it. Scoop rice onto cling wrap and shape into one big ball and two smaller ones.

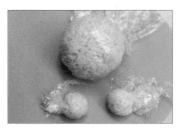

2. Cut a rectangular piece from an egg sheet and place it on the rice ball. Wrap in cling wrap to secure.

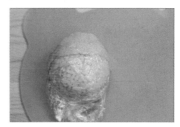

3. Fold a strip of egg sheet in half and make halfway cuts at half-inch intervals. Do not cut all the way.

4. Roll up the egg sheet and secure with a pasta stick. Use another pasta stick to attach it onto the girl's hair.

5. Punch out ovals from a sheet of nori using a nori punch. Cut out the girl's nose and mouth from nori using a pair of scissors.

6. Cut a round cucumber slice in half. Use a circle cutter to make a smaller round cut in a carrot. Then, cut it in half.

7. Dab on some mayonnaise as "glue" before placing sesame seeds on the carrot.

8. Assemble the girl in the bento box. Dab red cake decorating gel or ketchup on her cheeks using a chopstick.

Fall Squirrel

Fall is here when you see squirrels out in the gardens gathering acorns. Make this sandwich squirrel using a template. Learn to make acorns out of mushroom caps and hot dogs. Complete this fall-themed box with autumn leaves cut out from carrots.

BENTO MENU

Seafood aglio e olio
    (p. 233)
Tamagoyaki (p. 225)
Lettuce
Cherry tomato

FOOD ART INGREDIENTS

Brown egg sheet (p. 15)
Aburaage
Nori
Pink cake decorating gel
Cocktail sausage
Shimeji mushroom
Fried pasta sticks

TOOLS NEEDED

Parchment paper
Pencil/marker
Scissors
Knife
Tweezers
Craft punch
Autumn leaf cutter

1. When preparing an egg sheet, add soy sauce to the egg white to make a brown egg sheet. Using the template (p. 246), cut out the squirrel's body from the egg sheet and its hair and hairy tail from aburaage (p. 17). Alternatively, you can substitute aburaage with another egg sheet by adding more soy sauce to egg white to make it a darker brown.

2. Use a craft punch to cut out the eyes and nose from a sheet of nori. Use a pair of scissors to cut out two small curved lines for the mouth. Dab on pink cake decorating gel for the cheeks.

3. Slice off a piece of mushroom to form a cap. Slice a cocktail sausage in half. Using a fried pasta stick, attach the mushroom cap to the sausage.

4. Cut out autumn leaves from a slice of carrot using a leaf cutter.

Winter Girl

Brrrr...you know winter is here when it starts to get freezing cold. Keep warm in a thick hooded winter coat and gloves like the girl in this bento. Complete the winter-themed bento with snowflakes cut out from cheese. One of the side dishes in this bento is tamagoyaki, a rolled Japanese omelette that is soft and fluffy.

BENTO MENU	FOOD ART INGREDIENTS	TOOLS NEEDED
Chicken nuggets (p. 203)	Rice	Cling wrap
Tamagoyaki (p. 225)	Nori	Scissors
Carrots	Ketchup	Tweezers
Broccoli	Red bell peppers	Nori punch
Cherry tomato	Yellow bell peppers	Snowflake cutter
Lettuce	Cheese	

1. Mix ketchup with rice to color it. Using cling wrap, shape rice into a rice ball.

2. Make cuts along the edge of the bottom of a sheet of nori as shown. Continue to make cuts along the lines indicated in the picture. This will help mold the nori against the rice.

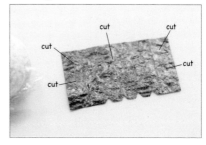

3. Place nori on the top portion of rice ball and wrap it with cling wrap. Set aside.

4. Using cling wrap, shape out a long strip of white rice for the lined fur in her parka.

5. Arrange the white rice onto the rice ball as shown. Use cling wrap to shape and mold the rice together.

6. Using a nori punch, cut out ovals in a sheet of nori for her eyes. Using a pair of scissors, cut out curved lines from the nori for her nose and mouth.

7. Using a pair of scissors, cut out her mittens from slices of red and yellow bell peppers.

8. Use a snowflake cutter to cut out snowflakes from a slice of cheese.

Raincoat Bear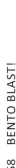

Rain, rain, go away, little children want to play! This teddy bear is all ready for the wet weather with his raincoat and umbrella. Using egg sheets, make a raincoat and an umbrella for teddy and brighten up your child's gloomy, rainy day.

BENTO MENU

Butter mushrooms (p. 230)
Salmon mayonnaise (p. 221)
Broccoli
Apples
Purple carrots

FOOD ART INGREDIENTS

Rice
Dark soy sauce
Egg sheet (p. 14)
Carrots
Pasta sticks

TOOLS NEEDED

Cling wrap
Knife
Hole punch
Tweezers
Umbrella handle pick
Circle cutter

1. Mix rice with dark soy sauce to color it. Using cling wrap, shape two brown rice balls—a big one for the head and a small one for the body. Using cling wrap, shape a small rice ball using white rice.

2. Place the white rice ball onto the bigger brown rice ball for the bear's snout. Wrap with cling wrap and mold them together.

3. Use a hole punch to cut out the eyes and nose from a sheet of nori. Use a pair of scissors to cut out a short straight line from nori for his mouth.

4. Cut out a piece from the egg sheet that is long enough to wrap around the bear's head. Fold the egg sheet in half before wrapping. Secure the egg sheet onto the rice ball using pasta sticks.

5. Cut out another piece of egg sheet and wrap it around the bear's body by folding it downward on both sides like a raincoat. Secure onto the rice ball using pasta sticks.

6. Assemble the bear in the bento box. Cut a circle from a slice of carrot using a round cutter. Use tweezers to place it onto the raincoat and secure using a pasta stick.

7. To make an umbrella, cut out a piece from the egg sheet. Prepare an umbrella handle pick and pasta stick.

8. Make pleats in the egg sheet by folding and secure with pasta sticks. Slot the bento pick into the egg sheet for the umbrella's handle.

Sunny Day by the Beach ☀

A smiley sun works hard on a blazing hot day as octopuses sunbathe at the beach under their umbrellas. The bread buns in this bento are filled with crab salad (made with imitation crab meat), but you can also replace it with tuna salad, egg salad, chicken salad, or whatever else you prefer.

BENTO MENU

Imitation crab meat
Mayonnaise
Bread buns
Broccoli pasta salad
    (p. 229)
Lettuce

FOOD ART INGREDIENTS

Cocktail sausages or hot
    dogs
Cheese
Nori
Sunny-side up egg
Carrots
Ketchup
Mayonnaise

TOOLS NEEDED

Knife
Round cutter or straws,
    one bigger and one
    smaller
Scissors
Tweezers
Nori punch
Heart-shaped bento picks
Cocktail umbrella picks
Chopstick

1. To prepare crab salad, slice imitation crab meat, mix with mayonnaise, and season with black pepper. Fill bread buns with lettuce and crab salad. Set aside.

2. Don't cook your cocktail sausages first. Slice off the ends of the cocktail sausages. You can also use hot dogs—just slice them shorter.

3. There are two ways to cut out your octopus sausages. Using a knife, make halfway cuts in the cross-section of the sausage as shown. Do not cut all the way.

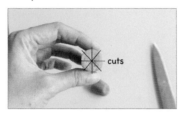

4. Boil the sausage until the ends curl up. This method of cutting is especially good if you want your octopus sausage to stand.

5. Another way of making an octopus sausage is by slicing off the end of the sausage diagonally, as shown, leaving a tip.

6. Using a knife, make three halfway cuts from the tip of the sausage.

7. Boil the sausage until the ends curl up. This octopus sausage can't stand on its own and can only be placed lying down.

8. Use a round cutter to cut circles from cheese for the eyes. To cut out a ring for the mouth, use two circle cutters or straws of different sizes—the outline of the smaller cutter should fit inside the larger cutter. First, make a cut in the cheese with the smaller cutter. Next, use the larger cutter to cut around this smaller circle to form the ring.

9. Using a nori punch, cut out eyes from a sheet of nori. Dab on some mayonnaise as "glue" before assembling the cheese and nori on the octopus with a pair of tweezers.

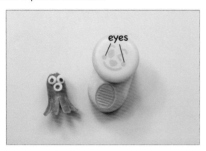

10. Using scissors, cut out sunglasses from a sheet of nori. Fold the nori in half and cut the shape of one side of the sunglasses along the folded edge, then open up the cutout.

11. Add a heart-shaped bento pick.

12. In your sunny-side up egg, use a round cutter large enough to cut around the circumference of the egg yolk while leaving a border of egg white.

13. Using a nori punch, cut out the eyes, nose, and mouth from nori. Use tweezers to place cutouts on the egg. Be careful when placing so that your yolk does not break.

14. Using a knife, slice out triangle shapes from carrots and arrange them around the egg yolk.

15. Arrange octopus sausages on the bread buns and add an umbrella pick.

16. Use a chopstick to dab ketchup on the egg yolk for the sun's cheeks.

Night Time

Twinkle, twinkle, little star, how I wonder what you are? Make a nighttime-themed bento filled with stars. An egg mold is used to form the star-shaped bread balls in this bento. Learn to make striped cheese by alternating dark and light colored cheese, and draw facial features on a banana skin using a toothpick to create a sleeping crescent moon. You can also use this method to create special messages or drawings on bananas for your kids.

BENTO MENU

Chicken teriyaki (p. 205)
Nutella sandwich
Carrots
Apples
Red currants

FOOD ART INGREDIENTS

Dark colored cheese
Light colored cheese
Bread
Nutella
Nori
Ketchup
Banana
Mayonnaise

TOOLS NEEDED

Cling wrap
Tweezers
Knife
Star cutter
Star-shaped egg mold
Craft punch
Chopstick
Toothpick

1. To make striped cheese stars, stack sliced cheese, alternating between dark and light colored ones. Leave at room temperature for a while so the layers melt and stick to each other.

2. Cut into half and stack them together.

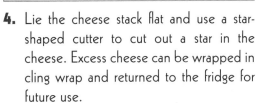

3. Slice out the block of cheese along its length into smaller sections.

4. Lie the cheese stack flat and use a star-shaped cutter to cut out a star in the cheese. Excess cheese can be wrapped in cling wrap and returned to the fridge for future use.

5. To make the bread ball, slice off crust from a slice of bread and roll the bread flat using a rolling pin.

6. Using a knife, make cuts along the edge of the bread as show in the picture. Place your desired fillings in the middle. Here, I use Nutella.

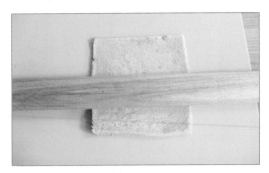

7. Gather the corners of the bread together.

8. Place bread into the egg mold and cover it firmly. Set aside for a while.

9. Remove the star-shaped bread from the egg mold.

10. Using a paw craft punch, cut out the star's eyes from a sheet of nori. Using a nori punch, cut out the star's mouth from the nori. Spread on a little mayonnaise as "glue" before using a pair of tweezers to place the nori cutouts onto the bread.

11. Use a chopstick to dab on ketchup for the star's cheeks.

12. Use a toothpick to carve the moon's features into the banana skin. Leave the banana aside for a while for the drawings to oxidize and show up clearly.

Bento and Food Art Tutorials

FOOD ART

Curry Polar Bear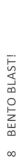

A polar bear, made from rice and nori, is taking a relaxing soak in a bowl of Japanese curry. Japanese curry is a breeze to cook at home with the help of instant curry roux, which you can buy at grocery stores. Japanese curry is suitable for kids as they come in mildly spicy versions. You can choose to replace beef with chicken for your curry. You can also replace curry with white wine chicken stew to make this pretty plate (p. 203). The flower in this bento is cut out from purple potatoes using the same the method used to cut carrot flowers.

BENTO MENU

Japanese beef curry
    (p. 202)

FOOD ART INGREDIENTS

Rice
Nori
Flower-shaped purple
    potatoes (p. 31, steps
    12–16)

TOOLS NEEDED

Cling wrap
Scissors
Tweezers
Hole punch
Cocktail umbrella pick
Flower-shaped cutter
Knife

1. Using cling wrap, shape out two long rice balls for the polar bear's hands and two small rice balls for his feet.

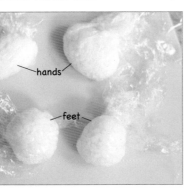

2. Using cling wrap, shape out one big rice ball for the polar bear's head and two small rice balls for his ears.

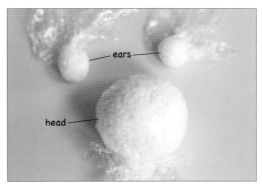

3. Using a hole punch, cut out six circles from a sheet of nori for the toes in his paw print. Use a pair of scissors to cut out two big circles from nori to complete the paw print.

4. Using a hole punch, cut out his eyes from nori. Using a pair of scissors, cut out a circle for his nose and a straight line for his mouth.

5. Scoop beef curry into a serving bowl. Arrange the rice balls and purple potato flowers on top.

6. Add an umbrella pick to shield him from the sun.

Swimming Ducky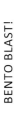

This little duck is just learning how to swim, so he stays afloat with the help of his little float. Craft him using rice and serve on top of a bowl of chicken milk stew. Milk stew is a healthier option compared to cream-based stew. This recipe uses miso (Japanese soy bean paste) for an extra unami taste.

BENTO MENU	FOOD ART INGREDIENTS	TOOLS NEEDED
Chicken milk stew (p. 211)	Rice	Cling wrap
	Hard-boiled egg yolk	Toothpick
	Carrot	Nori punch
	Nori	Knife
	Imitation crab meat	Tweezers
	Pasta sticks	Chopstick
	Pink cake decorating gel	

1. Using cling wrap, shape rice into a rice ball. Press with your fingers to mold a hole in the middle until a ring shape forms.

2. Use a toothpick to cut out the red strips from a cooked slice of imitation crab meat. Arrange it around the ring of rice.

3. Mix some rice with mashed egg yolk to color yellow.

4. Using cling wrap, shape yellow rice into a round rice ball for the head and an oval one for the body.

5. Using your hands, mold out the tip of the duck's tail in the oval rice ball.

6. Place rice balls together to see whether the size of the head corresponds to the size of the body. Shape it again if needed.

7. Using a pair of scissors, cut out the duck's bill from a slice of carrot.

8. Attach the carrot onto the rice ball using pasta sticks. Cut out the eyes from nori using a nori punch. Dab on cake decorating gel using a chopstick for the cheeks. Attach the head onto the body using pasta sticks.

Ham Piggy

Seafood aglio e olio is a delicious one-dish meal that you can whip up quickly. A ham piggy decoration on the top makes it even more attractive for the little ones. With the help of sandwich cutters, the piggy can be completed easily in less than 5 minutes. This dish and its decoration can also be easily packed into a bento box.

BENTO MENU

Seafood aglio e olio
(p. 233)

FOOD ART INGREDIENTS

Ham
Nori
Ketchup

TOOLS NEEDED

CuteZCute Animal
Friends cutter
CuteZCute Cuddle Palz
cutter
Tweezers
Nori punch
Chopstick

1. Here are the respective parts of each cutter that I will be using.

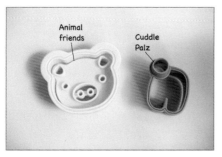

2. Cut out the piggy's head from a slice of ham using Animal Friends cutter.

3. Cut out the piggy's features from ham using the Animal Friends cutter.

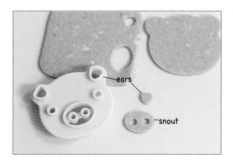

4. Cut out the piggy's body from ham using the Cuddle Palz body cutter. Use the circle on the body cutter to cut a small circle from the ham for the pig's tail in the next step.

5. Use a pair of scissors to cut around the curve of the circle to form the pig's curly tail.

6. Using a nori punch, cut out the pig's eyes and mouth from a sheet of nori.

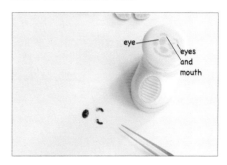

7. Dab on some ketchup using a chopstick for the cheeks.

Puff Pastry Soup Bear

Transform your boring bowl of soup into a work of art by serving it with a "puff pastry top hat." Puff pastry is the perfect match for a bowl of warm hearty soup with its complementary buttery, flaky textures. Plus, who wouldn't want to eat that?

BENTO MENU

Curry pumpkin soup
(p. 237)

FOOD ART INGREDIENTS

1 piece frozen puff pastry
1 egg, beaten
Water
Cheese
Nori
Ham
Pasta sticks

TOOLS NEEDED

Ramekin
Brush
Round cutters
Scissors
Tweezers

1. Cut out a circle in a piece of puff pastry big enough to cover the ramekin. Fill the ramekin with curry pumpkin soup. Brush the edges of the pastry with water to help seal it in the next step.

2. Place puff pastry over the ramekin and press down to secure the edges.

3. Cut out the bear's ears from the puff pastry using a round cutter, as shown.

4. Using a pastry brush, brush beaten egg all over the pastry covering the ramekin and the bear's ears. Bake at 350°F (180°C) for roughly 10–15 minutes.

5. Using a round cutter, cut out a circle from a slice of cheese.

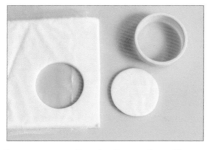

6. Cut out the bear's features from a sheet of nori using a pair of scissors.

7. Cut out two small circles from a slice of ham using a round cutter or straw for the bear's cheeks.

8. Assemble the parts onto the puff pastry and secure using pasta sticks.

Soup Kitty

This adorable kitty cat is trying to catch the yummy fish swimming in a bowl of asparagus soup. Kitty is shaped from mashed potatoes and the fish are made from toasted bread. This is great as a warm appetizer to fill your little one's tummy before the main meal.

BENTO MENU	FOOD ART INGREDIENTS	TOOLS NEEDED
Asparagus soup (p. 238)	Russet potato	Cling wrap
	Bread	Fish cutter
	Nori	Tweezers
	Pink cake decorating gel	Craft punch
	Butter	
	Salt	

1. Cut a large russet potato into small cubes and steam for around 12 minutes or until soft.

2. Mash potatoes using a fork. Add a pinch of salt and a half teaspoon of butter.

3. Shape the cat's body parts from the mashed potatoes and place on cling wrap.

4. Use a craft punch and a pair of scissors to cut out the cat's features from a sheet of nori. Dab on pink cake decorating gel for the cheeks.

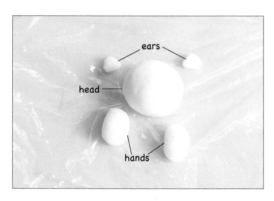

ears

head

hands

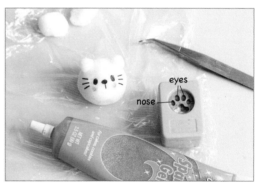

eyes

nose

5. Cut out the fish from a slice of bread using a small fish-shaped cutter. Toast in oven at 350°F (180°C) for 5 minutes. Arrange the cat and fish in the bowl of soup.

Tomato Soup Owl

Hoot! Hoot! Here's a cool way to serve your soup, by adding on an owl made out of wrap. The toasted wrap helps to make the soup more filling for hungry little tummies. This is great both as a side to a main meal or a midday snack.

BENTO MENU
Tomato soup (p. 238)
Parsley

FOOD ART INGREDIENTS
Tortilla wrap
Cucumber
Ham
Blueberries/black olives
Carrot

TOOLS NEEDED
Knife
Round cutter
Tweezers

1. Using a pair of scissors, cut out the owl's body and wings from a wrap. Place on a baking tray and toast in the oven at around 350°F (180°C) until crisp.

2. Slice the cucumber and then cut these round slices in half to form the owl's feathers.

3. Cut out circles in a slice of ham using a round cutter. Slice the circles in half.

4. Cut out a triangle from a slice of carrot for the owl's beak. Prepare two blueberries or small black olives for the owl's eyes.

5. Arrange the parts on the owl before placing it in a bowl of soup.

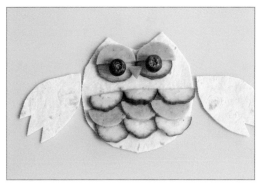

Pizza Bear

No time to make a full pizza? Well, just make an easy one using bread instead. The trick is to toast the bread before adding on the pizza toppings. Use a bear-shaped cutter to make this a time-saving recipe for your kids, and they will soon be asking for more! Pizza bears can also be packed in a bento box for your kids to bring to school.

BENTO MENU	FOOD ART INGREDIENTS	TOOLS NEEDED
Bread	Blueberries/black olives	CuteZCute Animal Palz
Ketchup/tomato paste/	Nori	cutter
pizza sauce	Cheese	Round cutters
Ham		Nori punch
Tuna		Tweezers
Mozzarella cheese		

1. Make a cut in a slice of bread using a bear cutter. Toast your bread on both sides for around a minute in a toaster oven.

2. Spread on ketchup, tomato paste, or pizza sauce. Add fillings like shaved ham, tuna, or anything you desire. Top with shredded mozzarella cheese. Return to the toaster oven and toast until the cheese melts.

3. You can also experiment with different sauce bases such as chicken bolognese (p. 235) or Japanese curry (p. 202).

4. Using a round cutter, cut out a circle from a slice of cheese for the bear's snout. Cut blueberries in half and use for the bear's nose. Attach onto the pizza bread using pasta sticks.

5. Use a nori punch to cut out the bear's eyes from nori. Cut out a strip of nori using scissors and use tweezers to place it under the bear's nose for the mouth.

6. You can also use olives in place of blueberries and nori for the bear's nose and eyes.

7. Pizzas can be made the day before and kept in the fridge. All you have to do is toast before serving the following day.

Animal Tortilla Chips

Kids love to snack on chips. Why not make your own healthier version? With the help of animal sandwich cutters, turn regular tortilla chips into cute animals. Serve these irresistible chips with salsa dip.

INGREDIENTS

Tortilla wrap
Salt
Salsa dip

TOOLS NEEDED

CuteZCute Cuddle Palz cutter
Baking paper

1. Using an animal sandwich cutter, make a cutout in a tortilla by pressing it hard on a flat cutting surface and moving the cutter to and fro.

2. Turn over tortilla to check that the cutter has fully cut through the tortilla before removing. You should see the cut outline of the animal's features.

3. Next, cut out the outline of the animal's face. Repeat with other animal cutters to create different animal-shaped tortillas.

4. Place the tortilla cutouts on a tray lined with parchment paper. Sprinkle on some salt. Bake them at 350°F (180°C) for 8 minutes.

5. Serve the chips with salsa dip.

Bento and Food Art Tutorials

BONUS FOOD ART RECIPES

Hot Dog Bread 🐷

INGREDIENTS

2 cups (250 g) bread flour

¼ cup (30 g) sugar

¼ tsp salt

2 tbsp (25 g) butter, at room temperature

1 tsp instant yeast

½ beaten egg (keep the remaining
   ½ egg for egg wash)

½ cup (120 g) water

Hot dogs

Raisins

Melted chocolate or a food marker

1. Mix bread flour, sugar, salt, yeast, egg, and water in a large bowl to get a dough. Add butter and knead for 10 minutes, until the dough is springy and soft. If you have a bread maker, use the dough function for steps 1 and 2.

2. Cover the dough with cling wrap and keep in a warm place for it to rise. This takes around an hour and the dough should double in size.

3. While the dough is rising, soak raisins in water so that they will soften and expand. Dry them on a paper towel and set aside. These will be for the doggies' noses.

4. Dust your worktable with some flour and place dough on it. Punch out the air from the dough with your fist.

5. Divide, roll out, and shape the dough into six large balls and six smaller ones. The big one will be the body and the small ones will be the head. Cover with cling wrap and let the dough rest for 15 minutes.

6. Roll out the big ball using a rolling pin. Place a hot dog in the middle. Fold the top and bottom of the dough over each other and seal by pressing the dough together. Turn the sealed part face down.

7. Seal one end and shape it into the tail, lightly twisting it and sealing it back against to the body.

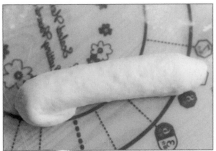

8. Make a "V"-shaped cut at the other end of the body to form the legs.

9. Lightly flatten the smaller ball of dough. Make two "V"-shaped cuts for the ears.

10. Place the head on the body. Cover with cling wrap and let the doggy proof—the final step before baking when the dough is left to rise even more—for 40 minutes.

11. At the end of 40 minutes, place the raisins into the face of the dogs and press gently.

12. To make egg wash, mix ½ beaten egg with 1 tbsp water. Brush the bread with egg wash and bake at 350°F (180°C) for around 15 minutes or until they turn golden brown. Draw eyes using melted chocolate in a piping bag or a food marker.

Steamed Chick Cake

INGREDIENTS

1 ½ cup (150 g) Morinaga pancake mix
2 small eggs
¼ cup (30 g) sugar
¼ cup (45 g) milk
¼ cup (45 g) plain yogurt

1 ½ tbsp (20 g) unsalted butter, melted
1 tsp baking powder
½ tbsp plain flour
½ tbsp cocoa powder
Orange gel-based food coloring

1. Whisk eggs and sugar in mixing bowl.

2. Add yogurt and milk until well blended.

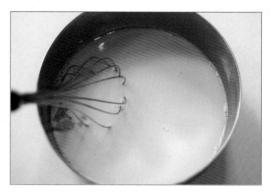

3. Stir in melted butter.

4. Sift in Morinaga pancake mix and baking powder and fold until well blended.

5. Scoop 1 tbsp of the batter made in step 4 and add ½ tbsp of dark cocoa powder. Mix well.

6. Scoop 1 tbsp of batter from step 4 and add ½ tbsp of flour. Add some orange coloring using a toothpick and mix well.

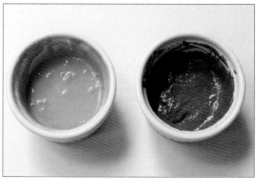

7. Spoon the colored mixtures made in step 5 and 6 into piping bags.

8. Fill cupcake cups with the remaining mixture that was not colored. Fill cups until around 70 percent full. Tap cups lightly to remove air bubbles.

9. Pipe on the chicks' details—draw their beaks using the orange batter and their eyes and feet using the brown batter.

10. Steam cupcakes in a preheated steamer on low heat for 12 minutes. While steaming, line the pot lid with a cloth on the inside to prevent water from dripping onto the cakes and spoiling the designs.

Note: If you can't get hold of Morinaga pancake mix, you can substitute it with 1 ½ cup (150 g) plain flour. Add 1 ½ tsp baking powder. Increase sugar amount to ¾ cup (80 g) and replace the yogurt with ⅓ cup (75 ml) milk instead.

Bunny German Cookies

INGREDIENTS

1 stick (125 g) butter
½ cup (50 g) icing sugar, sifted
⅔ cup (125 g) potato starch

⅔ cup (80 g) cake flour
Pink gel-based food coloring
Black sesame seeds

1. Beat butter and icing sugar until light and fluffy.

2. Sift in potato starch and flour. Mix until a soft dough is formed.

3. Scoop out 2 tbsp of the dough and mix in pink food coloring using a toothpick. Mix until the pink is evenly distributed.

4. Wrap both plain dough and pink dough with cling wrap and refrigerate for half an hour.

5. Remove dough from fridge. Roll the plain dough into balls, keeping a portion aside for the bunnies' ears and noses.

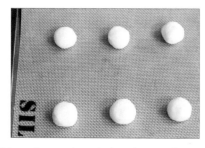

6. Take some plain dough from this leftover portion and shape the bunnies' ears. Attach to the balls of dough.

7. Use plain colored dough to roll out small ovals for the bunny's snout.

8. Use pink colored dough to roll out pink ovals for the cheeks.

9. Using tweezers, add black sesame seeds for the eyes and noses.

10. Bake at 320°F (160°C) for 15 minutes.

Steamed Piggy Buns

INGREDIENTS

2 cups (300 g) Morinaga pancake mix
1 ½ tbsp salad oil
¼–⅓ cup (90–100 ml) water
Pink gel-based food coloring
Cocoa powder

FILLINGS:

½ lb (250 g) boneless chicken thighs,
    cut to strips
1 tbsp oyster sauce
1 tsp soy sauce
1 tbsp sesame oil
1 tbsp Chinese rice wine
1 tbsp ginger juice
Pinch of salt
1 tbsp cornstarch
1 stalk scallion, chopped

1. Combine all ingredients for the fillings together and mix well using your hands. It is best to leave the meat to marinade overnight.

2. Sift pancake mix and add salad oil.

3. Add water gradually, using your hands to keep mixing until the dough comes together.

4. Scoop out 2 tbsp of dough and mix in pink gel-based food coloring using a toothpick. Keep kneading until the colors are even.

5. Scoop out 1 tbsp of dough and mix in cocoa powder. Keep kneading until the colors are even.

6. Dust work surface with flour. Use your hands to knead the remaining plain colored dough for around 5 minutes, until the dough becomes soft and smooth.

7. Divide dough into six parts and roll each into a ball. Use a rolling pin to flatten each ball.

8. Place fillings from step 1 in the middle of the dough. Wrap it up and pleat the edges to seal.

9. Turn it over and shape into an oval. Repeat for the other five balls.

10. Take the pink dough and shape out two rounded triangles for the ears. Use water to attach the ears onto the buns.

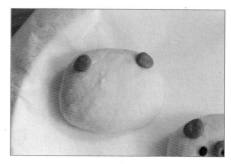

11. Take some pink dough and shape out an oval for the snout. Poke two holes in the snout using a straw. Use water to attach it onto the buns.

12. Take some brown dough and shape out circles for the eyes. Use water to attach the eyes onto the buns. Place the buns on wax paper and steam over low heat for 15 minutes.

Note: If you can't get hold of Morinaga pancake mix, you can also use 2 ½ cups (270 g) plain flour and 1 ½ tsp baking powder to ½ cup (140 ml) water. You need to add 3 tbsp of sugar and a pinch of salt as well. Cover the dough after step 7 and leave it for half an hour before you start rolling it out.

Bear Cream Puff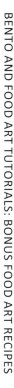

INGREDIENTS

For pâte à choux pastry:

½ cup (150 g) water
⅓ cup (100 g) milk
½ cup (125 g) unsalted butter
1 ¼ cup (150 g) plain flour
4 medium eggs
1 tbsp sugar
Pinch of salt

For crème pâtissière:

2 cups (500 ml) milk
4 egg yolks
1 cup (120 g) superfine sugar
4 tbsp cornstarch
1 tsp butter
1 tsp vanilla extract
Melted chocolate

To make crème pâtissière:

1. In a mixing bowl, add egg yolks, 4 oz (100 ml) milk, sugar, cornstarch, and vanilla extract in a bowl.

2. Heat the remaining milk to a scald in a saucepan. Pour the milk into the mixture in step 1, whisking continuously as you pour. Once incorporated, pour everything back into the saucepan.

3. Whisk mixture over medium-low heat. Keep stirring until it thickens. Remove from heat and whisk in butter.

4. Transfer the mixture to a bowl. Once it reaches room temperature, fill into a piping bag and refrigerate until ready to use.

To make pâte à choux pastry:

1. Heat butter, milk, water, sugar, and salt in a saucepan on low heat until the butter melts. Continue to bring to a boil and turn off the heat when it starts boiling.

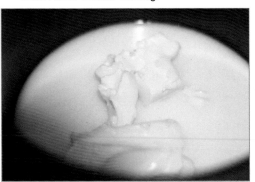

2. Remove saucepan from heat. Add sifted flour and mix well. Stir quickly until a dough is formed and it does not stick to the saucepan. If the mixture is still liquid, continue cooking on low heat until you get a dough.

3. Transfer the dough to another container. Use a wooden spatula to mix and cool down the mixture a little. Beat in the eggs one at a time using an electric mixer on low speed until the mixture is well combined and sticky.

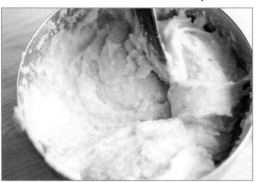

4. Transfer the mixture into a piping bag. Snip off the end and pipe out the bear on a baking sheet. Pipe out the body, followed by the ears.

5. Bake at 350°F (180°C) for 15 minutes. Do modify the time according to how your oven heats up. Once your puffs have risen to their maximum, you can turn down the temperature to 320°F (160°C) for another 25 minutes and continue baking until they are all golden brown.

6. Remove from the oven and let the puffs cool down. Poke a hole at the bottom of the puffs and pipe the crème pâtissière into the puffs. This way, they will be able to stand upright.

7. Draw the bear's features using melted chocolate.

PASTA AGNO OLIO
WITH SAUSAGES.

SALAD

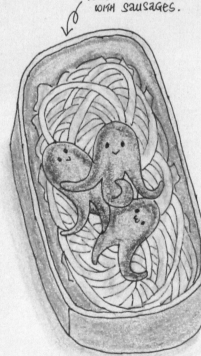

Recipes

MEAT

SEAWEED PORK ROLLS

INGREDIENTS

15 slices shabu-shabu pork
15 sheets nori (Japanese seaweed), cut slightly smaller than slice of pork
½ tsp salt
1 tbsp soy sauce
1 tbsp mirin
Flour/beaten egg/panko (Japanese bread crumbs) for coating

METHOD

1. Season pork slices with salt, soy sauce, and mirin.
2. Place a sheet of nori on top of a slice of pork.
3. Roll up the pork and nori.
4. Coat pork roll in flour, followed by egg, and finally with panko. Lightly press on panko and shake off excess.
5. Deep fry or shallow fry until golden brown.

JAPANESE BEEF CURRY

INGREDIENTS

½ lb (250 g) beef (shin or chuck tender), cut to bite sized chunks
1 onion, minced
1 carrot, cut into cubes
1 potato, cut into cubes
4 cubes Japanese instant curry roux
4 cups water

METHOD

1. Add beef to pan and brown both sides. Set aside.
2. Stir fry onions until soft and translucent.
3. Add beef, then add water and simmer until beef is soft and tender.
4. Add carrot and potato and simmer until they are soft.
5. Add curry roux cubes and stir until dissolved.
6. Adjust the consistency of the curry if needed. Simmer for a few more minutes if too watery or add water if the curry is too thick.

CHICKEN NUGGETS

INGREDIENTS

10 pieces chicken fillet, cut into pieces
½ small onion, chopped
2 cloves garlic, minced
1 tsp salt
1 tsp soy sauce
1 tbsp mirin
1 egg
Bunch of coriander, chopped
2 tsp cornstarch
4 cream crackers

METHOD

1. Place all the ingredients in a blender. Blend until chicken is ground and ingredients are well mixed. Set aside minced chicken paste for at least an hour.
2. Heat up oil. Use a spoon to scoop up minced chicken paste and drop it into the hot oil. Deep fry until golden brown.

WHITE WINE CHICKEN STEW

INGREDIENTS

½ chicken, cut into chunks
6 brown mushrooms, sliced
2 onions, cut into quarters
3 potatoes, chopped into cubes
1 small carrot, chopped into cubes
1 bay leaf
Salt and black pepper, to taste
1 tbsp unsalted butter
1 tbsp plain flour
1 cup white wine
1 cup hot water
1 cup chicken broth

METHOD

1. Lightly season chicken pieces with salt and pepper.
2. Add some oil to pan, dust chicken pieces with plain flour, and brown them on both sides. Set aside.
3. Add onions, potatoes, and carrot, and cook until onions soften. Then, stir in butter and flour until combined.
4. Add chicken, mushrooms, chicken broth, white wine, and bay leaf.
5. When the mixture comes to a boil, cover and simmer over low heat for around 20 minutes.

CHICKEN VEGGIE ROLL

INGREDIENTS

2 boneless chicken legs
¼ carrot, sliced into strips
8 asparagus spears/green beans
2 tbsp soy sauce
2 tbsp mirin
3 tbsp sake
2 tbsp sugar
⅔ cup water

METHOD

1. Slice carrots and cut off ends of asparagus. Blanch asparagus in boiling water.
2. Slice or pound chicken to make thickness of the meat the same. Place carrots and asparagus on top.

3. Roll up chicken and tie with string.

4. Heat up a pan with some oil and panfry chicken until all sides are browned.

5. Pour in water, followed by soy sauce, mirin, sake, and sugar. Simmer for 10 minutes.

6. Remove chicken rolls and cook remaining sauce until it thickens. Return chicken rolls back into pan and coat with sauce. Slice before serving.

CHICKEN TERIYAKI

INGREDIENTS

1 boneless chicken leg
2 tbsp soy sauce
2 tbsp mirin
2 tbsp sake
1 tsp sugar

METHOD

1. Poke chicken leg using a fork. This will help the marinade to penetrate better.
2. Marinade with soy sauce, mirin, and sake for an hour. Do not add the sugar yet.
3. Pat chicken dry using kitchen towels. Set aside the remaining marinade.
4. Heat up pan and fry chicken skin down until golden brown. Flip and cook on the other side until browned.
5. Wipe off oil in pan before pouring in the marinade from step 3 and sugar. Cook until chicken is well coated in sauce.

PORK NUGGETS

INGREDIENTS

1 lb (450 g) ground pork
1 small onion, cut into quarters
3 cloves garlic, peeled
4 cream crackers
2 tsp cornstarch
1 egg
Pinch of white pepper
1 tsp salt
2 tsp soy sauce

METHOD

1. Place all ingredients in food processor and blend everything together.
2. If the mixture is too dry, add 1 tbsp of water at a time until pork mixture is moist.
3. Lift and throw pork mixture in a bowl a few times. Leave it to marinade for an hour.
4. Heat up oil in pan, scoop pork mixture with spoon, and shape into a ball.
5. Fry until golden brown.

VEGGIE PORK/BEEF ROLLS

INGREDIENTS

10 slices shabu-shabu pork/beef (thinly
    sliced pork/beef)
½ carrot, peeled and cut into thin sticks
6 asparagus spears, ends trimmed and cut
    into half
Sea salt
Black pepper

Sauce:
3 tbsp soy sauce
3 tbsp mirin
2 tbsp sugar
2 tbsp sake

METHOD

1. Blanch sliced carrots and asparagus in
   boiling water for two minutes.
2. Sprinkle shabu-shabu pork with salt and
   black pepper. Place carrots and asparagus
   on pork and roll it up.
3. Heat oil in pan. Place pork rolls in pan
   with the seam line facing down. Panfry the
   pork rolls by rotating all sides until they are
   browned.
4. Mix ingredients for sauce together. Reduce
   heat and add sauce. Flip pork until they are
   well coated in sauce.

CHINESE PORK CHOPS

INGREDIENTS

1 lb (450 g) pork loin, cut to around
    ½-inch (1 cm) thick
2 tbsp soy sauce
1 tbsp oyster sauce
2 egg whites
1 cup bread crumbs

METHOD

1. Tenderize pork by pounding with a mallet
   or the back of a knife.
2. Marinade pork with soy sauce and oyster
   sauce for an hour.
3. Coat pork slices with egg whites and then
   coat with bread crumbs.
4. Heat up oil in pan. Panfry until one side
   is golden brown, before flipping over and
   frying until the other side is golden brown.

KETCHUP PORK CHOPS

INGREDIENTS

1 tbsp vegetable oil

2 cloves garlic, minced

½ red onion, cut into wedges

2 tbsp ketchup

1 tsp light soy sauce

¼ cup water

1 tsp sugar

1 tomato, cut into wedges

METHOD

1. Prepare pork chops following the Chinese pork chops recipe (p. 206).
2. Heat oil in wok. Stir-fry garlic and onion until onion wedges have softened.
3. Add the rest of the ingredients and bring to a simmer for around 2 minutes or until sauce is of a slightly thick consistency.
4. Pour sauce over pork chops before serving.

BROWN SAUCE PORK CHOPS

INGREDIENTS

1 ½ tbsp A.1. steak sauce

1 ½ tbsp HP Sauce

½ tbsp Worcestershire sauce

5 tbsp water

1 ½ tbsp sugar

1 tbsp cornstarch

METHOD

1. Prepare pork chops following the Chinese pork chops recipe (p. 206).
2. Mix the ingredients well.
3. Heat up pan, pour sauce into pan, and bring to a simmer.
4. Pour sauce over pork chops before serving.

GRILLED CHICKEN BALLS

INGREDIENTS

1 lb (450 g) chicken breast, cut into strips
5 stalks green onions, finely chopped
3 tbsp mirin
1 tbsp soy sauce
½ tsp salt
6 tbsp cornstarch
White sesame seed (optional)

Sauce:

2 tbsp soy sauce
2 ½ tbsp mirin
3 tsp sugar

METHOD

1. Mix chicken strips, green onions, mirin, soy sauce, salt, and cornstarch in a large bowl.
2. Using your hands, make small balls and place them on a lightly floured plate.
3. Heat a pan with some oil. Place chicken balls in the pan and cook until browned on both sides.
4. Mix ingredients for the sauce together and pour it in the pan. Turn the chicken balls so that they are well glazed. Turn off when more than half of the glaze has evaporated.
5. Remove chicken balls and pour remaining sauce on top. Sprinkle on white sesame seeds.

CAJUN SPICED GRILLED WINGS

INGREDIENTS

10 chicken wings
1 tsp salt
1 tsp garlic powder
2 tsp cajun spice mix
½ tsp black pepper

METHOD

1. Pat chicken wings dry with paper towels.
2. Place wings in a bowl. Add salt, garlic powder, cajun spice, and black pepper. Rub onto wings evenly using your hands. Leave to marinade for at least an hour.
3. Grill at 400°F (200°C) for 20 minutes.

CHICKEN CARROT STIR-FRY

INGREDIENTS

½ lb (250 g) chicken breast, cut into
   bite size
½ carrot, sliced
1 tsp minced ginger
Sauce:
4 tbsp chicken stock
Pinch of salt
Pinch of sugar
2 tsp sake
1 tsp cornstarch

METHOD

1. Blanch carrots in boiling water for 5 minutes.
2. Mix ingredients for sauce in a small bowl.
3. Heat up oil in pan. Stir-fry ginger until fragrant.
4. Add chicken and stir-fry until lightly browned.
5. Add carrots and stir-fry for 3 minutes.
6. Pour sauce in and stir-fry until sauce thickens.

CHICKEN SALAD

INGREDIENTS

1 chicken breast
½ tsp salt
1 tsp mirin
½ tsp black pepper
5 tbsp mayonnaise
Salt, to taste
Black pepper, to taste

METHOD

1. Marinate chicken for half an hour using salt, mirin, and black pepper. Cook chicken breast in boiling water. Remove and set aside. Reserve 5 tbsp of water from the water used to cook the chicken.
2. Shred chicken into pieces.
3. Mix well with mayonnaise and the water you reserved from step 1. Taste and season with salt and black pepper if needed.

CHICKEN TOFU PATTIES

INGREDIENTS

½ lb (300 g) ground chicken
¼ pound (140 g) tofu
1 inch ginger, minced
1 egg
3 stalks scallion, chopped

Marinade:
1 tbsp cornstarch

1 tbsp mirin
½ tsp salt
½ tsp soy sauce

Sauce:
4 tbsp soy sauce
4 tbsp mirin
2 tbsp sugar
4 tbsp water
1 tsp cornstarch

METHOD

1. Mix chicken, egg, ginger, and scallions with all marinade ingredients.

2. Drain tofu for 15 minutes. Pat tofu dry on kitchen towel.
3. Crumble tofu and mix with the mixture in step 1. Shape into patties.

4. Heat some oil in pan. Cook patties for around 5 minutes on one side, or until they are browned. Flip over and continue cooking for another 10 minutes on medium low heat. Remove and set aside.
5. Pour all ingredients for the sauce into a pan and bring to a boil. Add chicken patties to the pan and coat well in sauce.

CHICKEN MILK STEW

INGREDIENTS

2 chicken legs
¼ lb shimeji mushrooms, ends trimmed
½ carrot, sliced into cubes
1 potato, sliced into cubes
½ cup broccoli florets
1 ¾ cups milk
2 cups water
½ onion, sliced thinly
1 clove garlic, minced
2 tbsp miso
Salt, to taste
Black pepper, to taste
2 tbsp plain flour
1 tsp dill

METHOD

1. Marinate chicken with a little salt and black pepper. Add flour to chicken.
2. Heat oil in pan. Panfry chicken until it is lightly browned. Set aside.
3. Heat oil in pan. Add garlic and onion and sauté until fragrant.
4. Add potato, carrot, and mushrooms. Stir-fry for 2 minutes.
5. Add milk and water, bring to boil, then turn dial to simmer.
6. Add dill. Continue to simmer for 10 minutes. Then, add in miso paste using a sieve.
7. Add chicken and simmer for 5 minutes.
8. Add broccoli and simmer for another 3 minutes. Season with salt and black pepper, if needed.

GROUND PORK AND POTATO STIR-FRY

INGREDIENTS

¼ lb (80 g) ground pork
½ onion, minced
2 cloves garlic, minced
1 russet potato, peeled and sliced ¼-inch (½ cm) thick

Marinade:
½ tsp light soy sauce
½ tsp sesame oil
1 tbsp Chinese rice wine
½ tbsp cornstarch
Dashes of white pepper

Sauce:
1 cup water
1 tbsp light soy sauce
½ tbsp dark soy sauce
1 tsp sesame oil

METHOD

1. Mix all marinade ingredients and marinade pork for 10 minutes.
2. Heat up pan with a little oil. Add onions and stir fry until translucent.
3. Add garlic and give a few quick stirs.
4. Add pork. Stir-fry and break into small pieces.
5. Add potato and sauce. Simmer until sauce almost runs dry and potatoes are soft.

LEMON CHICKEN

INGREDIENTS

½ lb (300 g) boneless chicken breast/chicken
   leg, cut into small pieces
½ tsp white sesame seeds
½ cup cornstarch

Marinade:

1 tbsp soy sauce
1 tbsp Chinese rice wine
1 tbsp cornstarch

Sauce:

6 tbsp lemon juice
4 tsp sugar
10 tbsp water
2 tsp cornstarch
Pinch of salt

METHOD

1. Marinade chicken pieces with marinade for 30 minutes.
2. Mix all ingredients for sauce and set aside.
3. Coat chicken pieces with cornstarch before deep frying until golden brown. Place chicken pieces on paper towels.
4. Add sauce ingredients to a pan and bring to boil.
5. Transfer chicken pieces to sauce and coat well.
6. Top with sesame seeds before serving.

TONKATSU

INGREDIENTS

½ lb (200 g) pork loin, sliced into half
1 tsp salt
1 tsp black pepper
Plain flour
Egg, beaten
Panko (Japanese bread crumbs)

METHOD

1. Pound pork loin using a meat pounder or the back of your knife.
2. Dust with salt and black pepper.
3. Dredge meat in flour and remove excess. Dip in egg mixture. Finally, dredge in panko and remove excess. Press panko gently onto the meat.
4. Deep fry until golden brown.

BLACK PEPPER CHICKEN

INGREDIENTS

1 boneless chicken breasts, cut into strips
2 tbsp oil
1 onion, sliced
1 red bell pepper, cut into strips
1 tsp black pepper
2 tbsp soy sauce
Pinch of sugar

METHOD

1. Marinade chicken strips with 1 tbsp of soy sauce.
2. Heat up oil in skillet. Add onion and stir-fry until aromatic.
3. Add bell pepper and black pepper. Stir-fry for 1 minute.
4. Add chicken. Stir-fry until chicken is cooked.
5. Add remaining soy sauce and sugar. Stir to combine well.

CHICKEN VEGGIE STIR-FRY

INGREDIENTS

½ lb (250 g) chicken breast, cut into cubes
1 tsp cornstarch
2 tsp oil
1 clove garlic, minced
1 cup broccoli florets
½ cup red bell pepper, cut into cubes
½ cup yellow bell pepper, cut into cubes

Sauce:
½ tbsp oyster sauce
1 tsp soy sauce
3 tbsp water
Dash of white pepper
1 tsp sugar
1 tsp rice vinegar
1 tsp sesame oil
1 tsp cornstarch
Salt to taste

METHOD

1. Marinade chicken with 1 tsp cornstarch for 5 minutes.
2. Mix all ingredients for the sauce and set aside.
3. Heat up skillet with oil. Add garlic and stir-fry a few times.
4. Add chicken and stir-fry until the surface turns white.
5. Add broccoli and bell pepper. Stir to combine well before adding the sauce.
6. Continue to stir-fry until the sauce thickens.

HONEY CHICKEN

INGREDIENTS

½ lb (250 g) chicken breast/leg, cut
    into pieces

Cornstarch mixture—2 tsp cornstarch to
    4 tsp water

Marinade:

½ tsp salt

Dash of white pepper

Honey garlic sauce:

⅓ cup honey

1 clove garlic, minced

1 tsp salt

1 tsp Chinese rice wine

1 tsp vinegar

¼ cup water

METHOD

1. Marinade chicken pieces for 5 minutes.
2. In a bowl, mix together all ingredients except garlic to make the honey garlic sauce. Set aside.
3. Heat oil in wok, coat chicken pieces in cornstarch, and drop in hot oil. Deep-fry until the pieces turn golden brown.
4. Remove and drain on paper towels.
5. Add 2 tbsp of oil to wok. Stir-fry garlic pieces until browned. Remove garlic pieces and discard.
6. Add sauce to wok and bring to a light simmer. Add cornstarch mixture to thicken the sauce.
7. Add chicken pieces and toss until they are well coated in sauce.

MEAT SOBORO

INGREDIENTS

½ lb (200 g) ground pork/chicken
1 tsp minced garlic
1 tsp minced ginger
1 tbsp sugar
1 tbsp sake
1 tbsp dark soy sauce (optional)
3 tbsp oyster sauce
Pinch of salt

METHOD

1. Mix all ingredients together, except garlic. Set aside for at least 15 minutes. If needed, add some water to loosen up the ground meat.
2. Heat up pan with some sesame oil and stir-fry garlic.
3. Add meat mixture. Keep stirring and breaking up the meat until the liquid is almost dried up.

CRISPY CHICKEN FILLET

INGREDIENTS

1 skinless chicken breast
1 clove garlic, peeled
Zest from 1 lemon
10 cream crackers
2 tbsp olive oil
8 sprigs of fresh Italian parsley
Sea salt and black pepper to taste
¼ cup flour
1 egg

METHOD

1. Slice chicken breast into two pieces. Pound them with the back of a knife until they are around the same thickness.
2. Put crackers, oil, parsley, lemon zest, garlic, sea salt, and black pepper in a food processor. Blend until you get a fine mixture. Pour the crumbs onto a plate.
3. Dip the chicken in flour, then into egg, and finally coat them well with the crumbs from step 2.
4. Heat up a pan with oil. Shallow fry your chicken in a pan until one side is golden brown. Flip and remove when the other side turns golden brown.

PORK CARROT PATTIES

INGREDIENTS

1 lb (400 g) ground pork
½ carrot, shredded and chopped
½ onion, minced
1 egg
1 tsp salt
1 tsp soy sauce
1 tsp garlic powder
½ cup bread crumbs
Dash of pepper

METHOD

1. In a large bowl, mix together all ingredients. Set aside for half an hour.
2. Shape mixture into patties.
3. Heat up a pan with oil. Fry patties until one side is browned. Flip over and fry until the other side is brown.

PORK CABBAGE STIR-FRY

INGREDIENTS

½ cabbage, chopped
½ lb (200 g) pork, thinly sliced
1 tbsp garlic, minced

Sauce:
2 tbsp soy sauce
2 tbsp sake
1 tbsp sugar
1 tbsp miso

METHOD

1. Mix all ingredients for the sauce in a bowl. Set aside.
2. Heat up a pan with a little oil. Stir-fry garlic until aromatic.
3. Add pork. Sauté until it changes color.
4. Add sauce.
5. Add cabbage. Sauté until the cabbage wilts and is well coated in sauce.

JAPANESE HAMBURG STEAK

INGREDIENTS

½ large onion, minced
Pinch of salt and 1 tsp salt
Pinch of black pepper and 1 tsp black pepper
½ lb (200 g) ground beef
½ lb (200 g) ground pork
1 egg
2 tbsp milk

⅓ cup panko

Sauce:
4 tbsp soy sauce
4 tbsp mirin
2 tbsp sugar
4 tbsp water
1 tsp cornstarch

METHOD

1. In a bowl, pour milk over panko. Set aside for panko to soften and expand.
2. Heat oil in a pan and sauté the onion until translucent. Season with a pinch of salt and black pepper. Transfer to a bowl and let it cool.
3. Add the meat in the bowl with egg, 1 tsp salt, 1 tsp black pepper, panko mixture from step 1, and onions from step 2. Mix well using your hands.

4. Shape into patties. Toss patty from one hand to another repeatedly for about 5 times to release air inside the mixture.

5. Keep the patties in the fridge for 30 minutes before cooking.
6. In a large pan, heat oil over medium heat and place the patties gently in the pan. Indent the center of each patty with 2 fingers because the center of patties will rise with heat.
7. Cook until one side is browned. Flip and continue cooking until the other side is browned.

8. Reduce to low heat. Cover and cook for 5 minutes.
9. Pour in sauce, turn heat back to medium, and cook until sauce thickens.

Recipes

SEAFOOD AND EGG

KETCHUP SHRIMP

INGREDIENTS

10 large shrimp
2 cloves garlic, minced
1 inch ginger, grated
4 tbsp ketchup
1 tbsp mirin
1 tbsp sake
Pinch of sugar

METHOD

1. Peel, shell, and devein shrimp.
2. Heat oil in pan over medium heat. Add garlic and ginger, and sauté until fragrant.
3. Add shrimp to pan and stir-fry until it changes color (the inside of the shrimp does not have to be cooked through at this point).
4. Add ketchup, mirin, sake, and a pinch of sugar. Stir well until shrimp are fully cooked and well coated in sauce.

FRIED SALMON BELLY FINGERS

INGREDIENTS

1 lb (400 g) salmon belly
1 tsp of salt
½ tsp of pepper
1 egg
1 cup cornmeal

METHOD

1. Cut salmon belly into strips.
2. Season salmon belly with salt and pepper.
3. Beat the egg. Dip salmon belly strips in egg, followed by cornmeal.
4. Deep-fry or panfry until golden brown.

GARLIC SHRIMP

INGREDIENTS

10 medium shrimp
10 cloves garlic, minced
2 tbsp olive oil
½ tsp sea salt
Black pepper to taste

METHOD

1. Wash, peel, and devein shrimp.
2. Heat up pan with olive oil. Add minced garlic and sauté for a minute.
3. Add shrimp and sauté them. Add sea salt and black pepper.
4. Remove once shrimp are cooked.

CRISPY FRIED SHRIMP

INGREDIENTS

12 medium shrimp

Marinade:

1 tsp salt
1 tsp sesame oil
Dash of pepper
1 tbsp Chinese rice wine

Batter:

1 cup all-purpose flour
2 tsp baking powder
2 tbsp potato flour
½ tsp salt
1 tbsp sesame oil
¼ cup cold water

METHOD

1. Wash, shell, and devein shrimps with tails intact. Make a few cuts in the abdomen to break the veins if you want the shrimp to stay straight, instead of curving, after frying.
2. Add seasoning and leave for 30 minutes.
3. Sift flour for batter and mix well with the rest of the batter ingredients.
4. Heat up oil in wok. Coat shrimps in batter and deep fry until golden brown.

SALMON MAYONNAISE

INGREDIENTS

2 salmon fillets
½ tsp sea salt
2 tbsp mayonnaise
1 tsp lemon juice

METHOD

1. Rub both sides of salmon fillets with salt.
2. Arrange in a dish and cover . Refrigerate for an hour.
3. Preheat oven to 400°F (200°C). Bake for around 6 minutes. Flip salmon and bake for another 4 minutes.
4. Mix mayonnaise with lemon juice and spread onto salmon. Return to the oven and cook for another 2 minutes.

CHEESY FISH FILLET

INGREDIENTS

2 slices white fish fillet
Pinch of salt
Pinch of black pepper
1 egg
2 tbsp Parmesan cheese
Flour

METHOD

1. Slice fish fillet into thinner slices. Season with salt and black pepper.
2. Add Parmesan cheese to egg. Mix well.
3. Heat pan with a little oil. Coat fish fillet with flour and shake off excess. Dip in egg mixture and panfry until one side is golden brown. Flip over and fry until the other side is golden brown.

SALTED SALMON

INGREDIENTS

½ lb (250 g) salmon
½ tbsp sake
3 tsp salt

METHOD

1. Slice salmon. Pour and spread sake on salmon. Let rest for 10 minutes.
2. Pat dry salmon using a kitchen towel.
3. Apply salt on the salmon, adding more on the skin.
4. Place salmon on a tray lined with paper towels. Leave in the fridge overnight.
5. Bake in oven at 400°F (200°C) for around 20 minutes, or until flesh is firm and skin is crispy.

LEMON SOY SAUCE SALMON

INGREDIENTS

½ lb (250 g) salmon
1 tbsp sake
1 ½ tbsp soy sauce
1 tbsp lemon juice
Pinch of sugar

METHOD

1. Slice salmon. Pour and spread sake on salmon. Leave for 10 minutes.
2. Pat dry salmon using paper towels. Mix soy sauce, lemon juice, and sugar, then set aside.
3. Heat some oil in pan. Panfry salmon until both sides are browned.
4. Place salmon on a plate and drizzle soy sauce mixture over salmon.

LEMON DILL SALMON

INGREDIENTS

2 salmon fillets

Seasoning:
Pinch of sea salt
Pinch of black pepper
1 tsp salted butter

Seasoned butter:
1 tsp fresh dill, chopped
½ tsp garlic powder
Zest of one lemon
1 tbsp salted butter, softened at room
    temperature

METHOD

1. Prepare seasoned butter by mixing all ingredients well. Set aside.
2. Rub salmon with salt and black pepper.
3. Spread some plain butter on salmon and grill until cooked.
4. Top with seasoned butter from step 1 just before serving.

CHEESE BAKED SHRIMP

INGREDIENTS

8 large shrimp
2 tbsp butter, softened
2 tbsp minced garlic
Mozzarella cheese, grated
Pinch of salt
Dash of pepper

METHOD

1. Mix butter, garlic, salt, and pepper in a bowl. Set aside.
2. Wash and clean shrimp. Partially remove shells from the body, leaving the head and tail intact. Make a slit in the back of each shrimp.
3. Stuff mixture from step 1 into the slit and top shrimp with mozzarella cheese.
4. Bake at 350°F (180°C) until shrimp are cooked and cheese is browned.

SCRAMBLED EGGS

GREEN BEAN OMELETTE

INGREDIENTS

2 eggs
1 tbsp butter
2 tbsp milk
Pinch of salt
Dash of black pepper

METHOD

1. Beat eggs, milk, salt, and black pepper in bowl until foamy on top.
2. Heat butter in pan over medium heat.
3. Pour in egg mixture. As eggs begin to set, keep pulling the eggs with your spatula, forming large, soft curds.
4. Continue doing so until eggs thicken and almost no liquid remains.

INGREDIENTS

3 eggs, beaten
1 tsp light soy sauce
Dash of white pepper
10 green beans, ends trimmed and sliced thinly
5 garlic cloves, minced
Pinch of salt

METHOD

1. Mix eggs, white pepper, salt, and soy sauce in a small bowl.
2. Heat oil in pan. Fry minced garlic until light brown.
3. Add sliced green beans and stir-fry for a minute.
4. Pour egg mixture over the beans. Cook a few minutes on one side until nicely browned, before flipping to the other side.

TAMAGOYAKI

INGREDIENTS

2 eggs

Seasonings:
1 tsp mirin
½ tsp soy sauce
1 tbsp water

2 tsp mayonnaise
Pinch of sugar

TOOLS NEEDED

Tamagoyaki pan or square pan

METHOD

1. Gently mix the eggs in a bowl. In another bowl, combine the seasonings and mix well. Pour all seasonings into the egg and whisk gently.
2. Strain egg mixture through a sieve.
3. Heat a tamagoyaki pan over medium heat. Apply oil to the pan with a paper towel.
4. Once pan is hot, pour a thin layer of egg mixture in the pan, tilting to cover the whole pan.
5. Once the bottom of the egg has set and is still soft on top, start rolling from one side to the other—in this case, from left to right.

6. Keep the omelette to the right side where you had rolled it to. Apply oil to the pan with a paper towel.

7. Pour egg mixture to cover the whole pan again. Lift the rolled omelette to spread the egg mixture underneath.

8. When the bottom of the new layer has set and is still soft on top, start rolling the omelette in the opposite direction, from right to left. You can brown the omelette a little.

9. Remove from pan. Place omelette on bamboo mat and wrap it up. Shape egg when it's still hot. Leave for 5 minutes.

10. Slice before serving.
11. For scallion tamagoyaki, add chopped scallion to egg mixture after straining in step 2.

Recipes

VEGETABLES

SESAME BROCCOLI

INGREDIENTS

1 ¼ cups (200 g) broccoli spears
2 tbsp sesame oil
1 clove garlic, minced
1 tbsp toasted sesame seeds
¼ tsp salt

METHOD

1. Blanch broccoli in boiling water (with 1 tsp of salt added) for not more than 2 minutes.
2. Remove broccoli from boiling water and immediately plunge it into ice water.
3. Drain broccoli well. Add the rest of the ingredients to the broccoli and toss well.
4. This dish can be chilled before serving.

ZUCCHINI AND TOMATO BAKED WITH CHEESE

INGREDIENTS

1 medium zucchini, chopped
1 tomato, diced
3 cloves garlic, minced
Pinch of sea salt
Pinch of black pepper
⅓ cup parsley, finely chopped
½ cup Parmesan cheese, shredded

METHOD

1. In a mixing bowl, add all ingredients except parsley. Lightly stir to combine.
2. Transfer to a baking dish and bake in preheated oven at 350°F (180°C) for around 30 minutes.
3. Garnish with parsley before serving.

BELL PEPPERS STIR-FRY

INGREDIENTS

½ red bell pepper, seeds removed, cut into strips
½ orange/yellow bell pepper, seeds removed, cut into strips
1 tbsp sesame oil
1 tbsp soy sauce
2 tbsp mirin
Pinch of sugar

METHOD

1. Heat pan with sesame oil.
2. Add bell pepper and stir-fry for 2 minutes.
3. Add soy sauce, mirin, and sugar. Stir-fry until sauce almost dries up.

SQUASH STIR-FRY

INGREDIENTS

½ cup (80 g) squash, skin removed, cut into
   strips
1 tbsp sesame oil
1 tbsp soy sauce
2 tbsp mirin

METHOD

1. Heat pan with sesame oil.
2. Add squash. Stir-fry for two minutes.
3. Add soy sauce and mirin. Stir-fry until sauce almost dries up.

SRIRACHA ASPARAGUS

INGREDIENTS

1 ½ cups (250 g) asparagus
1 tbsp cooking oil
1 clove garlic, minced

Sauce:
1 tbsp sriracha chilli
1 tsp sesame oil
1 tsp fish sauce

METHOD

1. Trim and discard the lower ends of asparagus. Peel out the outer skin using a vegetable peeler and discard.
2. Heat oil in wok. Stir-fry garlic until fragrant.
3. Add asparagus, followed by sauce. Stir-fry for a few minutes until the asparagus is cooked.

POTATO SALAD

INGREDIENTS

½ Japanese cucumber, cut into thin slices
½ carrot, cut into thick slices
2 russet potatoes, peeled and quartered
¾ cup Japanese mayonnaise
Salt and pepper to taste

METHOD

1. Rub cucumber with salt and set aside for 30 minutes. Rinse well, drain, and pat dry with kitchen towels.
2. Add carrot and potatoes to boiling water and boil for 10 minutes. Drain.
3. Set carrots aside. Mash up potatoes, leaving some small chunks behind.
4. Add potatoes, carrots, and cucumbers to a bowl. Mix in Japanese mayonnaise and season with salt and black pepper. Chill in fridge before serving.

BROCCOLI PASTA SALAD

INGREDIENTS

1 cup (100 g) farfalle pasta
¾ cup (100 g) broccoli, cut into small
   florets
5 tbsp mayonnaise
1 tbsp sugar
1 tbsp red wine vinegar
Pinch of salt
Chili flakes (optional)

METHOD

1. Cook pasta in a pot of boiling water with 1 tbsp salt added until al dente. Drain and set aside.
2. Cook broccoli in boiling water for 2 minutes. Remove and plunge into ice water. Drain and set aside.
3. Mix together mayonnaise, sugar, vinegar, and salt.
4. Pour dressing over pasta and broccoli. Mix well. Sprinkle chili flakes, if desired. Chill in fridge before serving.

GREEN BEANS AND MUSHROOM STIR-FRY

INGREDIENTS

2 cups (250 g) green beans, trimmed
1 cup (150 g) mushrooms, sliced
1 tbsp cooking oil
½ onion, thinly sliced
1 clove garlic, minced
1 tsp grated ginger
1 tbsp oyster sauce
2 tbsp water
Pinch of sugar

METHOD

1. Blanch green beans in boiling water for 3 minutes.
2. Heat wok with a little oil. Stir-fry onion until soft. Add mushrooms and stir-fry for 3 minutes.
3. Add garlic and ginger. Stir-fry for a minute.
4. Add green beans, oyster sauce, sugar, and water. Stir-fry for another minute.

BUTTER MUSHROOMS

INGREDIENTS

2 cups (250 g) mushrooms
2 tbsp unsalted butter
1 tbsp minced garlic
½ tsp salt
½ tsp black pepper

METHOD

1. Melt butter in a pan over low heat.
2. Add garlic and stir-fry for a minute, until fragrant.
3. Add mushrooms, salt, and black pepper.
4. Stir-fry until mushrooms are cooked.

SOY SAUCE OKRA

INGREDIENTS

10 okra pods
2 tsp soy sauce
1 tsp lemon juice

METHOD

1. Cook okra in boiling water for 2 minutes.
2. Drain and let them cool slightly.
3. Slice them diagonally. Mix well with soy sauce and lemon juice.

BROCCOLI AND CARROT STIR-FRY

INGREDIENTS

1 clove garlic, finely chopped
3 slices ginger
1 cup broccoli florets
½ medium carrot, sliced into strips
2 tbsp oyster sauce
Pinch of sugar
Cornstarch mixture—½ tsp cornstarch to 1 tbsp water

(Besides carrots, cauliflower or mushrooms can also be used.)

METHOD

1. Heat up oil in wok. Sauté garlic, followed by ginger.
2. Add carrots and stir-fry for around 2 minutes. Add in water, 1 tbsp at a time, if needed for a slightly wetter consistency.
3. Add broccoli and stir-fry for 3 minutes. Add oyster sauce and sugar. Add water, 1 tbsp at a time, if needed for a slightly wetter consistency.
4. Add cornstarch mixture. Remove from heat once sauce thickens.

SESAME SPINACH

INGREDIENTS

6 cups (200 g) baby spinach
Salt, to taste
1 tbsp toasted sesame seeds
½ tbsp sesame oil
1 clove garlic, minced

METHOD

1. Blanch spinach in a pot of water, with 1 tsp salt added, for 30 seconds.
2. Remove spinach and immediately plunge into ice water until cooled.
3. Use your hands to squeeze out excess water from the spinach.
4. In a bowl, add spinach and the rest of the ingredients. Mix well.

PEA SHOOTS AND MUSHROOM STIR-FRY

INGREDIENTS

1 cup (150 g) pea shoots
1 ½ cups (100 g) mushrooms, sliced
1 garlic clove, minced
2 tbsp chicken or vegetable broth
Pinch of salt

METHOD

1. Heat up the oil in a pan. Stir-fry garlic until aromatic.
2. Add mushrooms and stir-fry for 2 minutes.
3. Add pea shoots and broth and stir-fry until just wilted.
4. Season with salt.

ASPARAGUS AND CORN STIR-FRY

INGREDIENTS

¾ cup (100 g) asparagus, ends trimmed and sliced diagonally
¼ cup (50 g) baby corn, sliced diagonally
1 clove garlic, minced
1 tbsp minced ginger

(Besides corn, mushrooms can also be used.)

Sauce:

1 tbsp soy sauce
1 tbsp fish sauce
1 tbsp sugar
¼ cup water

METHOD

1. Mix all ingredients for the sauce in a bowl. Set aside.
2. Heat up pan with a little oil. Stir-fry garlic and ginger until aromatic.
3. Add asparagus and corn and stir-fry for 2 minutes. You can also add mushrooms if you like.
4. Add sauce and simmer for a minute.

Recipes

NOODLES AND SOUP

CHICKEN CARBONARA

INGREDIENTS

Olive oil
1 chicken breast, sliced into small pieces
1 tbsp garlic, minced
1 tsp salt
1 tbsp plain flour
2 clove garlic, minced
1 ¼ heavy cream
½ cup grated Parmesan cheese
2 tsp parsley, chopped
1 egg yolk
5 strips bacon
2 servings pasta

METHOD

1. Season chicken breast with ½ tsp of salt.
2. Fry bacon until crisp. Remove and set aside.
3. Bring a pot of water with 1 tbsp sea salt added to boil. Cook until pasta is al dente. While pasta is cooking, whisk together cream, cheese, and parsley.
4. Heat up frying pan with a little olive oil. Coat chicken with flour and panfry until both sides are browned. Remove and set aside.
5. Heat up frying pan with a little olive oil, add garlic, and stir-fry until fragrant. Add bacon, chicken, and pasta. Toss to combine.
6. Add cream mixture and toss to combine over medium-low heat, until sauce thickens.

SEAFOOD AGLIO E OLIO

INGREDIENTS

Olive oil
2 servings of pasta
10 cloves garlic, chopped
2 tbsp butter
5 tbsp white wine
10 large shrimp
1 squid, cut into rings
1 bunch of parsley, chopped
1 tsp dried chili flakes
Sea salt and black pepper, to taste

METHOD

1. Bring a pot of water, with 1 tbsp sea salt added, to boil. Cook pasta until al dente.
2. Remove shells, heads, and veins from shrimp. Set aside the shrimp shells and heads.
3. Add butter in a saucepan. Panfry shrimp until lightly charred. Remove and set aside.
4. Add olive oil to saucepan. Add garlic and sauté until light brown. Add shrimp shells and heads and stir-fry until they change color. Discard once they are cooked.
5. Add white wine to deglaze.
6. Add squid and stir-fry until almost cooked.
7. Add pasta and toss well.
8. Add shrimp, chili flakes, and parsley. Toss to coat all ingredients. Season with sea salt and black pepper.

MEATBALL PASTA

INGREDIENTS

1 lb (400 g) ground beef

12 cream crackers

5 sprigs fresh rosemary, leaves plucked and finely chopped

2 tbsp dijon mustard

Olive oil

1 egg

1 tsp sea salt

1 tsp black pepper

1 onion, finely chopped

1 bunch of fresh basil, leaves picked

2 cloves garlic, minced

6 cups canned diced tomatoes

2 tbsp balsamic vinegar

2 servings pasta

Parmesan cheese, grated

METHOD

1. Pulse cream crackers in a food processor until fine.
2. Add beef, mustard, rosemary, sea salt, black pepper, crackers, and egg to a mixing bowl. Mix well using your hands.
3. Scoop mixture and roll into meatballs. Drizzle and coat them with olive oil. Cover and leave in fridge.
4. Cook pasta in water with 1 tbsp of sea salt added until al dente. Remove, drain, and set aside. Reserve 5 tbsp of pasta water.
5. Heat pan with olive oil and panfry meatballs until golden brown. Remove and set aside.
6. Heat pan with olive oil and stir-fry onion until softened. Add garlic and stir-fry until fragrant.
7. Add tomatoes and balsamic vinegar. Taste and season with salt and black pepper.
8. Add meatballs to sauce and simmer for 10 minutes.
9. Add pasta and pasta water reserved from step 4. Toss well.
10. Sprinkle basil leaves and grated Parmesan over the dish.

CHICKEN BOLOGNESE PASTA

INGREDIENTS

½ yellow onion, diced

½ carrot, peeled and chopped

½ celery stalk, chopped

1 cloves garlic, minced

1 lb (250 g) ground chicken

½ cup dry white wine

1 can (15 oz) crushed tomatoes

½ cup chicken stock

1 tablespoon fresh parsley (optional)

¼ teaspoon dried thyme

¼ cup milk

¼ cup grated Parmesan cheese

1 tablespoon fresh basil, chopped

Salt and pepper to taste

2 servings spaghetti

Grated Parmesan cheese for garnish

METHOD

1. Heat oil in a pan. Add the onion, carrot, and celery, and sauté until softened, about 5–7 minutes. Add garlic and cook for another minute.
2. Add chicken and cook, breaking up the pieces, until there is no pink remaining, about 5 minutes.
3. Add wine, increase the temperature to high, and boil for 2 minutes.
4. Add tomatoes and their juice, chicken stock, parsley, and thyme and bring to a boil.
5. Reduce the heat to low and simmer for 1 hour, uncovered, until the sauce has slightly thickened. In the last 10 minutes, add the milk, Parmesan cheese, and basil, and season with salt and pepper.
6. Serve on top of the cooked spaghetti and garnish with Parmesan cheese.

Note: This sauce tastes even better the next day. It can be made up to 2 days in advance. It freezes well.

PAD THAI

INGREDIENTS

1 ½ cups (100 g) rice noodles
1 tbsp oil
1 clove garlic, finely minced
⅓ pound (100 g) medium-sized shrimp, shelled
    and deveined
½ cup (50 g) firm tofu, cut into slices
1 egg
½ cup (50 g) bean sprouts
4 stalks of Chinese chives, cut into 2-inch lengths
2 tbsp crushed peanuts
Lime wedges

Sauce:

1 ½ tbsp fish sauce
1 ½ tbsp sugar
2 tbsp water
1 tbsp rice vinegar
1 tsp chilli powder

METHOD

1. Boil rice noodles following package instructions. Remove noodles and rinse under cold running water.
2. Mix all ingredients for the sauce and set aside.
3. Heat up wok and add oil. Add garlic and stir-fry until fragrant.
4. Add the shrimp and tofu. Continue stir-frying until the shrimp change color.
5. Add noodles and continue to stir-fry for a minute.
6. Push the noodles to one side. Crack an egg in the empty side of the wok. Use a spatula to break up the egg yolk and mix with the egg white. Cook for a minute. Combine the egg with the noodles.
7. Add the sauce. Stir to combine well with the noodles.
8. Add bean sprouts and chives. Stir in crushed peanuts once bean sprouts are cooked.
9. Dish out and serve with lime wedges.

PESTO PASTA

INGREDIENTS

2 servings pasta noodles
1 ¼ cup (60 g) basil leaves
5 stalks parsley leaves
2 cloves garlic, peeled
⅓ cup (30 g) toasted pine nuts
¾ cup (60 g) Parmesan cheese
½ cup extra virgin olive oil
Salt and pepper to taste

METHOD

1. Blend basil, parsley, garlic, pine nuts, and cheese until well combined.
2. With the blender motor still on, gradually pour in oil until you get a thick and smooth consistency.
3. Season with salt and pepper. Set aside.
4. Add 1 tbsp of salt to boiling water. Cook pasta until al dente. Reserve 2 tbsp of pasta water.
5. Toss pasta with pesto and leftover pasta water.

CURRY PUMPKIN SOUP

INGREDIENTS

4 cups (500 g) pumpkin, cut into cubes
½ cup chicken stock
1 tsp curry powder
1 tbsp butter
½ cup onion, chopped
½ cup heavy cream
½ cup milk
1 tsp salt

METHOD

1. Melt butter in pan. Add onion and cook to soften.
2. Add pumpkin and stir-fry for a minute.
3. Pour in chicken stock and curry powder. Bring to boil and simmer for 15 minutes.
4. Let mixture cool down a little before pureeing in a blender.
5. Return blended mixture to stove. Add heavy cream and milk. Bring to boil.
6. Season with salt.

ASPARAGUS SOUP

INGREDIENTS

6 cups (800 g) asparagus
1 large onion, chopped
3 tablespoons unsalted butter
5 cups chicken broth
½ cup heavy cream
¼ teaspoon lemon juice
Salt to taste
Black pepper to taste

METHOD

1. Cut tips from asparagus and chop the rest into 1-inch pieces.
2. Heat a pot over medium heat. Melt butter and add onion. Cook until onion softens, stirring regularly.
3. Add asparagus and cook for 5 minutes, stirring regularly.
4. Add chicken broth and simmer with pot covered until asparagus pieces are tender, about 15 minutes.
5. Remove from heat. Blend using an immersion blender until smooth.
6. Return to the pan over medium heat. Stir in heavy cream.
7. Season with salt and black pepper.
8. Add lemon juice.

TOMATO SOUP

INGREDIENTS

1 tbsp butter
1 large onion, finely chopped
1 clove garlic, smashed and peeled
2 cups chicken stock
1 28-oz can tomatoes, pureed
1 sprig fresh thyme
½ tsp sugar
Salt and pepper to taste
2 tbsp of sliced basil

METHOD

1. Melt butter in pan. Add onion and garlic and cook until softened.
2. Add tomatoes, stock, sugar, and thyme and bring to boil. Simmer for 30 minutes.
3. Discard the thyme sprig. Let mixture cool down a little before blending in a blender.
4. Return blended mixture to stove. Add basil and season with salt and black pepper.

Glossary

ABURAAGE

Aburaage, a fried tofu pouch, is a Japanese food product made from soybeans. It is made by cutting tofu into thin slices and then deep-frying them. Aubraage is often used to wrap inari-zushi—sushi rice stuffed in seasoned aburaage tofu pouches—and is also added to dishes such as miso soup and udon.

Where to buy: Specialty Japanese grocery stores

BONITO FLAKES

Bonito flakes are savory flakes of dried, smoked bonito fish, a type of tuna. They look similar to wood shavings. The flakes are used to make dashi, a seasoning in many Japanese dishes, and can also be used as fillings in onigiri (rice balls).

Where to buy: Japanese grocery stores or online retailers

CAKE DECORATING GEL

Cake decorating gels are ready-made piping gels that are sold in tubes and that come in different colors. The gels are transparent and are used to decorate and draw on cakes and cookies. A famous brand cake decorating gel brand is Wilton, which is what I use. See also *gel-based food coloring*.

Where to buy: Baking supplies stores

CHEESE

In this book, I make references to using dark or light colored cheese to make different elements in food art. Dark colored cheese refers to cheese that is a darker orange than the average light colored yellow cheese. An example of dark colored cheese that I use is cheddar, and a light colored cheese that I use is Monterey Jack. You can choose any type of dark or light colored cheese at your grocery store.

Where to buy: Any grocery store

CHINESE EGG NOODLES

Chinese egg noodles are a type of wheat based noodle. Although they vary in terms of thickness, I used the thicker kind of Chinese egg noodles in this book, which are denser and less springy. Egg noodles are often used in stir-fried noodle dishes with a heavy or rich sauce. Chinese egg noodles can be substituted with spaghetti.

Where to buy: Specialty aisles in grocery stores

CURRY POWDER

Curry powder is a spice mix that varies widely in composition based on the cuisine it is used in. Yellow curry powder, which contains turmeric, can be used to color food such as eggs in this book's food art recipes.

Where to buy: Any grocery store

DECO-FURI

Deco-furi is a kind of colored rice seasoning. It adds both colors and flavors to plain rice, making it very useful for character bento making. See also *pink sushi mix* and *sakura denbu*.

Where to buy: Japanese grocery stores or online retailers

FISH SAUCE

Fish sauce is a savory, flavorful sauce that is an important condiment in Southeast Asian cooking. The distinctive flavor in Thai dishes such as pad thai is attributed to the use of fish sauce. Fish sauce is made using anchovies, salt, and water.

Where to buy: Specialty aisles in grocery stores

GEL-BASED FOOD COLORING

A concentrated gel typically used for coloring icing. It only takes a very small amount to color your icing without thinning it down. Gel-based food colorings can be used for bento making too, for example to help you color foods like quail eggs (p. 16), mashed potatoes (p. 177, steps 1 and 2), and egg sheets (p. 14). See also *cake decorating gel.*

Where to buy: Baking supplies stores

IMITATION CRAB MEAT

Imitation crab meat, also known as crab sticks, is a type of processed seafood made from a white fish called surimi that has been shaped and cured into strips. A layer of red food coloring is added in stripes on the outside to resemble the leg meat of a snow crab. This cheaper alternative for crab can be found in sushi, such as California rolls. For the purposes of food art, imitation crab meat used in this book can be substituted with the skin of red bell peppers.

Where to buy: Specialty aisles in grocery stores

JAPANESE CUCUMBER (KYURI)

Japanese cucumber, or kyuri, is thinner than the Western cucumber. They are always eaten unpeeled and are commonly found raw in salads, as a garnish, or pickled in an iced brine. Japanese cucumbers that are used in the food art recipes in this book can be substituted with the thicker Western cucumbers instead—just slice them into smaller pieces using cutters or a knife.

Where to buy: Japanese grocery stores

JAPANESE HAMBURG STEAK

Japanese hamburg steak is a popular Japanese lunch item that draws inspiration from the Western hamburger and the Salisbury steak. It is a thick ground meat patty (usually a blend of ground beef, pork, and other ingredients) that is panfried and served with a sauce. Usually, it is not eaten with buns, but with rice instead.

How to make: Follow the step-by-step recipe (p. 217).

JAPANESE INSTANT CURRY ROUX

Japanese instant curry roux is the premix version of Japanese curry, a thick, non-spicy curry that is one of the most popular dishes in Japan. Instant curry roux contains curry powder, flour, oils, and seasonings, and is available in cubes that can be dissolved and cooked in water, making preparation easy and convenient.

Where to buy: Specialty aisles in grocery stores
How to make: Follow the step-by-step recipe (p. 202).

JAPANESE MAYONNAISE

Japanese mayonnaise and American mayonnaise are very similar, but the presence of a few different ingredients gives Japanese mayonnaise a different flavor and consistency. Japanese mayonnaise is creamier in color and texture due to its use of egg yolks instead of whole eggs. It is also sweeter and a little tangy since it uses rice vinegar instead of distilled vinegar. The most popular Japanese mayonnaise brand is Kewpie Mayonnaise. To substitute for Japanese mayonnaise, add 2 tbsp of rice vinegar and 1 tbsp of sugar to one cup of American mayonnaise and whisk until the sugar dissolves.

Where to buy: Japanese grocery stores or online retailers

JAPANESE SEAWEED/NORI

Nori is a type of seaweed that is widely used in Japanese cuisine. There are three types of nori: yaki nori (dry-roasted), ajitsuke nori (seasoned and roasted), and tsukudani nori (wet seasoned). Nori is used to wrap onigiri (rice balls) and sushi for a textural crunch. Dry-roasted nori is most suitable to be used in making the smaller details in character bentos—it cuts easily with nori punchers and can store well in an airtight box with a desiccant.

Where to buy: Specialty aisles in grocery stores

MAKI SUSHI

Maki sushi is a type of sushi roll that consists of nori rolled around vinegar-flavored rice and various fillings, which can include raw seafood, egg, vegetables, etc. Maki means "roll." Maki sushi can be a thick roll with a few ingredients, or a thin roll with just one ingredient.

MATCHA (GREEN TEA POWDER)

Matcha is finely milled high-quality green tea that comes in the form of a fine powder. Besides being used to brew tea, matcha can also be used to flavor and color food.

Where to buy: Japanese grocery stores or online retailers

MIRIN

Mirin is an important condiment in Japanese cooking. It is a sweet cooking wine made by fermenting sweet glutinous rice with a distilled alcoholic beverage, but has a low alcohol content and a high sugar content. Mirin tenderizes and adds a mild sweetness to meat dishes. It also helps to mask the smell of fish and seafood, and adds luster to ingredients. To substitute mirin, you can add 1 tsp of sugar to 1 tbsp of white wine. It won't be exactly the same, but it is an acceptable alternative.

Where to buy: Japanese grocery stores

MISO

Miso is a traditional Japanese seasoning made from fermented soybeans. It is one of the main ingredients used to make miso soup. It can be used to season many dishes.

Where to buy: Specialty aisles in grocery stores

MORINAGA PANCAKE MIX

Morinaga is a popular brand of pancake mix from Japan that lets you make perfectly fluffy pancakes.

This mix can also be used to create a variety of foods such as steamed cakes, steamed buns, donuts, etc. If you can't get Morinaga pancake mix, you can create a substitute with plain flour, baking powder, and various other ingredients, which I detail in the individual recipes (p. 189, 194).

Where to buy: Japanese grocery stores or online retailers such as Marukai eStore

ONIGIRI

Onigiri, or rice ball, is a Japanese food made from white rice that has been formed into triangular or oval shapes, and then wrapped in nori. Onigiri was originally devised as a way of using leftover cooked rice and making it portable and easy to carry around. For the purpose of food art, onigiris will help you make cute characters.

OYSTER SAUCE

This is a rich, savory sauce made from boiled oysters and other seasonings is a staple in Chinese cooking. It is used to flavor meat and vegetables, and is commonly used in noodle stir-fries.

Where to buy: Specialty aisles in grocery stores

PANKO

Panko is Japanese-style bread crumbs that is made from crustless bread. It is coarsely ground into large, airy flakes that give fried food a light, crunchy coating. It is often used in Japanese dishes like tonkatsu (p. 212). The flakes tend to stay crispier longer than standard bread crumbs because they don't absorb as much grease.

Where to buy: Specialty aisles in grocery stores

PINK SUSHI MIX

Pink sushi mix is a colored rice seasoning. It has the taste of ume, a pickled Japanese plum, and can be mixed into your rice to create sushi rice. Pink sushi mix also allows you to produce pink colored rice for the purposes of creating food art. See also *deco-furi* and *sakura denbu*.

Where to buy: Japanese grocery stores or online retailers

QUAIL EGGS

Quail eggs are tiny eggs with a speckled shell. They are considered a delicacy in some parts of the world. In Japanese cuisine, they are sometimes used raw or cooked as tamago, a Japanese omelette, that is packed in bento lunches. They can be sold fresh or canned.

Where to buy: Specialty aisles in grocery stores

RICE NOODLES

Rice noodles are noodles that have been made using rice flour. They are more fragile and delicate than wheat noodles, and come in a few different varieties. The rice noodles used in this book for the pad thai (p. 236) are flat and thin, similar to linguine.

Where to buy: Specialty aisles in grocery stores

RICE VINEGAR

Rice vinegar is vinegar that has been made from rice. Its taste is milder, less acidic, and sweeter than Western vinegars. If you cannot get hold of rice vinegar, you can substitute it with white wine vinegar that has been diluted with water and mixed with a little sugar.

SAKE

Sake is an alcoholic beverage from Japan that is made from rice and water. Sake has a higher alcoholic content and lower sugar content compared to mirin. Just like white wine, sake can be used for cooking and is often present in marinades for meat and fish to tenderize them and mask their smells. Sake also adds body and flavor to soup stock and sauces, and it's used in dishes like chicken teriyaki (p. 205). If you cannot find sake, substitute it with dry sherry or white wine.

Where to buy: Specialty aisles in grocery stores

SAKURA DENBU

Sakura denbu is a sweet and salty pink-colored flaked fish condiment that is used to season and color plain rice in sushi rolls or other rice dishes. It is usually sold in packets. See also *deco-furi* and *pink sushi mix.*

Where to buy: Japanese grocery stores or online retailers

SESAME OIL

Sesame oil is a fragrant vegetable oil derived from sesame seeds. It is mostly used as a flavor enhancer in cooking.

Where to buy: Specialty aisles in grocery stores

SESAME SEEDS

Sesame seeds are tiny, flat oval seeds harvested from the flowering plant sesame. Sesame seeds add a nutty taste to many Asian dishes. They are rich in minerals and are also a rich source of oil. Black sesame seeds and white sesame seeds, which refer to the seeds that are hulled, both appear in this book.

Where to buy: Specialty aisles in grocery stores

SHABU-SHABU PORK

Shabu-shabu is a hot pot dish from Japan, during which diners cook an assortment of raw vegetables and meat in a savory boiling broth. Shabu-shabu pork refers to ready sliced raw pork that is pre-packed and sold in grocery stores. They tend to be very thinly sliced cuts of meat that would cook very quickly once immersed in the shabu-shabu hot pot. As an alternative, use a marbled or fatty cut of pork that is thinly sliced.

Where to buy: Japanese grocery stores

SHIMEJI MUSHROOM

Shimeji mushrooms are small mushrooms that come in clusters. They have a white base and cracked, speckled brown caps. They taste a little bitter raw and are usually eaten cooked. They are also called beech mushrooms because they often grow on fallen beech trees.

Where to buy: Specialty aisles in grocery stores

SOBORO

Soboro is a crumble-like topping served on top of plain rice to season and flavor. The toppings can be made from ground meat, fish, eggs, etc. In Japan, families usually make tricolor soboro, which can consist of a meat soboro made from ground chicken, an egg soboro, and a green vegetable soboro made from green peas or spinach. Soboro can also be used as onigiri fillings.

How to make: Follow the step-by-step recipes (p. 215).

SOY SAUCE

Soy sauce is one of the most important condiments and seasonings in Chinese and Japanese cooking. Soy sauce is extracted from a fermented paste made from soybeans, wheat, salt, and yeast.

There are two types of soy sauce, light soy sauce (also commonly called soy sauce) and dark soy sauce. Light soy sauce is thin, lighter in color, saltier, and adds a distinct flavor to food. Dark soy sauce is darker, slightly thicker, less salty, and slightly sweet. It is used to add color and flavor to a dish.

Where to buy: Specialty aisles in grocery stores

SPAGHETTI AGLIO E OLIO

Spaghetti aglio e olio is a garlic and oil spaghetti dish that originates from Italy. This simple Italian pasta dish is made by lightly sautéing minced garlic in olive oil, sometimes with dried red chilli flakes, and tossing it with spaghetti.

How to make: Follow the step-by-step recipes to make a seafood variation (p. 233).

SPAM MUSUBI

Spam musubi originates from Hawaii. It consists of a slice of grilled Spam on top of a block of rice, wrapped together with nori. Spam musubi is a popular snack and lunch food.

How to make: Follow the step-by-step recipes (p. 62).

TAMAGOYAKI

Tamagoyaki literally means "grilled egg." It is a type of sweet Japanese omelette, made by rolling together thin layers of egg until you get a solid piece of rolled up egg. Tamagoyaki is usually served as one of the dishes in a Japanese-style breakfast and is a bento box staple in Japan. It can also be served on top of sushi.

How to make: Follow the step-by-step recipes (p. 225).

TAMAGOYAKI PAN

Tamagoyaki is usually prepared in a rectangular omelette pan, called a tamagoyaki pan. You can use any square-shaped pan to cook tamagoyaki. If you can't find one, you can use a small, round pan, and simply trim off the edges of the tamagoyaki to make it rectangular.

Where to buy: Online retailers such as Bento&co

TOFU

Tofu is made from soybeans, water, and a coagulant or curdling agent. Tofu is high in both protein and calcium, a good alternative to meat dishes.

Where to buy: Any grocery store

TONKATSU

Tonkatsu, or Japanese pork cutlet, is a fried breaded pork loin. It is usually eaten with a thick Worcestershire sauce and served with shredded cabbage and rice.

How to make: Follow the step-by-step recipes (p. 212).

TURMERIC POWDER

Turmeric powder, a South Asian spice, is yellow in color and can be used to coloring and flavoring food.

Where to buy: Specialty aisles in grocery stores

WASHI TAPE

Washi tapes are decorative Japanese paper tapes that are great for papercraft, gift wrapping/ packaging, scrapbooking, etc. In this book, they are used to create patterns and flags in bento boxes.

Where to buy: Japanese stores or online retailers

Templates

Acknowledgments

I would like to thank my husband, Thomas, for letting me indulge in this bento hobby. I want to thank my two boys, Ivan and Lucas, who are always willing to eat any character bentos I make, including more girl-themed ones. I would like to thank my family—especially my sister, Li Hui—for their support and encouragement.

I would also like to thank Kimberley Lim from Skyhorse Publishing for contacting me to write this book, helping me along, patiently answering all sorts of questions, and editing this book.

I'm just a mother who enjoys making food cute for my two boys. I'm very thankful to all my readers for their support in my bento making journey. And to you—thank you very much for picking up this book. I really hope it will be useful in your very own bento making journey.

Last but not least, I would like to thank the following companies, for kindly providing part of the bento boxes and tools that I used in this book.

BENTO USA .COM

Bento&co

EasyLunchboxes
Pack Lunches Fast!

monbento

black+blum

About the Author

Ming is a mother to two boys. She started making character bentos when her oldest son was facing separation anxiety during his first years of elementary school. She hoped to ease his anxiety by giving him something to look forward to during lunchtime at school. She has since created over 1,000 character bentos for her two boys over the span of four years. She shares her bentos on her blog, www.bentomonsters.com, as well as on Instagram, instagram.com/bentomonsters, which has since received an overwhelming response of 245,000 followers. Her character bentos have been featured on *New York Post, The Huffington Post, Daily Mail, Today,* and many other news sites around the world.